Home Exteriors

A Do-It-Yourselfer's Guide

Home Exteriors
A Do-It-Yourselfer's Guide

Drs. Carl and Barbara Giles

TAB BOOKS

Blue Ridge Summit, PA

FIRST EDITION
FIRST PRINTING

© 1992 by **TAB Books**.
TAB Books is a division of McGraw-Hill, Inc.

Library of Congress Cataloging-in-Publication Data

Giles, Carl H.
    Home exteriors : a do-it-yourselfer's guide / by Drs. Carl and
Barbara Giles.
        p.   cm.
    Includes index.
    ISBN 0-8306-1973-9   ISBN 0-8306-1953-4 (pbk.)
    1. Siding (Building materials)—Amateurs' manuals. 2. Exterior
walls—Amateurs' manuals. 3. House construction—Amateurs' manuals.
4. Dwellings—Remodeling—Amateurs' manuals. I. Giles, Barbara,
1944-.
    TH2231.G55 1991
    698—dc20   91-19097
                                              CIP

TAB Books offers software for sale. For information and a catalog, please contact
TAB Software Department, Blue Ridge Summit, PA 17294-0850.

Acquisitions Editor: Kimberly Tabor
Book Editor: Lori Flaherty
Book Design: Jaclyn J. Boone
Director of Production: Katherine G. Brown
Cover: Holberg Design, York, PA   TAB1

Contents

This book is dedicated to those consumers and corporations who are working to help preserve and protect what wildlife and their (our!) environment is left in America and the rest of the world. Two of those organizations that are most dedicated to saving them are The Animals in Advertising Association and The North American Wildlife Center, Inc.

Acknowledgments

We wish to thank the following people for their assistance in helping us to compile the information we needed to complete this book:

Spaceplan is one of the finest architectural firms in the Southeast. Operated by Carroll Hughes, it is progressive, permits only the highest quality, and does some of the finest work in America. Alan Sutton, also of Spaceplan, was most helpful.

Dataproducts Laser Printer Model 1260, the number one choice of printers, is the fine laser printer that helped us to produce the manuscript for this book. Product Manager John Paul Jones was instrumental in getting the LZR delivered to us.

Without the quality and dependability of Husqvarna, manufacturers of superior chain saws and tractors, we would have been even more pressed in meeting our deadline. A special thanks to Mark Michaels, Husqvarna product manager.

The Earl Raiford Lumber Co., Asheville, North Carolina, was most helpful in furnishing information on cedar, redwood, and other lumber. Raiford Lumber President Robert Wenige is one of the most informed authorities on sidings in the nation.

Ryobi America Power Tools were very helpful in showing us how different brands of saws, drills, and other tools performed on sidings. Not surprisingly, Ryobi products excelled in every instance. (And we are looking forward to seeing its new cordless circular saw perform!)

Many others were a great help in furnishing information and art for this book: Wolverine Technologies; Stucco Stone, Inc.; Red Devil, Inc.; AmeriMark; EZ Paintr; CertainTeed Monogram Vinyl Siding; Glidden

Paints; Barricade Building Wrap; and Thermo-Ply Sheathing. They are to be applauded.

Finally, we would be remiss if we failed to thank Ben Ogden, Montana cowboy, North Carolina mechanic, and wildlife worker, who helped to keep the Wildlife Center running while we worked on this book.

Introduction

Any wall in a private residence or business building will have two surfaces: the interior wall covering and the exterior wall covering. Siding is the exterior wall covering that presents the house to public view.

The most common types of siding are bricks, vinyl, aluminum, shakes of cedar or similar wood, boards, hardboard, and plywood. All types of siding can be installed by the do-it-yourselfer. Some require more expertise and more equipment, while others require only a hammer, saw, nails, and a few other basic carpentry tools.

The type of siding that a homeowner chooses to install will vary with the climate, type of house, geographic area, and the tastes of the individual. Some homeowners will install siding to make the house more economical to heat and cool, while others think more in terms of aesthetics, increased value of the house, or physical needs particular to that family or part of town. Even the amount of spare time the do-it-yourselfer has at his disposal might figure into the type of siding chosen.

Brick siding probably requires more expertise and time than any other type, while vinyl siding is among the fastest types of siding to install. Some of the basic plywood sidings require considerable physical work, helpers, or ingenuity, but the processes of installation are among the simplest.

This book is for those do-it-yourselfers who want to know what is on the market for their needs, how much knowledge is required to install the preferred type of siding, what the major advantages and disadvantages of certain types of siding are, and what the relative costs of installation are.

This book does not detail a dollars and cents cost; these figures are subject to rapid change and might become outdated within weeks after publication. The emphasis is instead placed on ratio or proportional cost, such as one type of siding might cost more than twice that of another, rather than actual amounts. When figures are given, they will be used only to reflect relative costs at the time of installation.

Home Exteriors: A Do-It-Yourselfer's Guide, covers the many types of sidings available and how to install them. You'll learn how to save money by trading your spare time and energy for home improvements at the lowest possible costs and with the best available workmanship—your own.

There are several specific reasons for the popularity of siding and do-it-yourself installation. Any business recession tends to make the average person more dollar-conscious, and there is a reluctance to expend large sums of money when the economic future is cloudy.

Older houses (the average house in the United States is 24-years-old) that are weather-beaten and in danger or deterioration can be easily revitalized. These older houses can be updated while they are being beautified, and the result of a good siding job can be a more valuable home as well as a more attractive structure.

Contracted installation of siding might cost $20,000, but the do-it-yourselfer can easily save $10,000 or more of that cost by doing the work himself. Even if he must hire a helper, he can still save half of the labor cost.

The high cost of new housing often makes it economically more feasible to upgrade an older house than to buy a new one. In 1988, for example, a $150,000 house loan at the lowest possible interest rates required a $1,300 monthly repayment rate for a 30-year mortgage. Many younger couples are unable to secure such a loan or have reservations about making the mortgage payments.

Housing figures reveal that the typical one-family house has 2,200 square feet of siding on it. Three billion feet of forest products are used annually in remodeling and new house construction. Half of this amount is devoted to exterior plywood. Factory-finished hardboard runs a close second in popularity to plywood.

Brick and vinyl sidings enjoy considerable popularity, with aluminum, stone, concrete blocks, and shakes or shingles, or combinations of two or more of the previous, accounting for the majority of other siding materials. Products like Masonite are also used frequently.

Siding installation is generally regarded by realtors and bankers as sound investments. The cost of do-it-yourself installation is affordable, and loans are often available for 65 percent up to 100 percent of the total cost. Building contractors often voice the opinion that a good siding job will pay for itself quickly, either in increased value of the house or in the savings on heating and cooling and the lack of maintenance.

Board or clapboard sidings, which were extremely popular many years ago, are still used, but many homeowners are moving away from this type of material today. The reasons often cited include the need to scrape, caulk, renail, and paint too often. While some of the non-wood siding materials used today might not have to be repainted at all or only require infrequent touch-up.

Some sidings need no maintenance at all. Others, like vinyl and aluminum, require only periodic washings rather than painting. When you install your own siding, you can save, on the average, half of the cost of a contracted job. With many types of construction work, labor usually accounts for 50 percent of the total cost.

Some siding materials can be installed directly over existing exterior walls. It is possible to easily cover walls of clapboard, bricks, plywood, or cement blocks.

Basic siding work requires careful attention to details, such as precise measurements, following directions carefully, cutting exactly to length and as instructed, and working in alcoves, around corners, or at windows and doors. You do not need to possess any highly technical knowledge, nor do you have to be an expert builder in order to install siding.

You'll learn what tools are needed for each particular job and what other equipment is necessary.

When practical, some estimates relative to installation time are provided. Of course, these will vary with the individual do-it-yourselfer in terms of his amount of help, physical limitations, and level of experience.

Instructions are given in simple, easy-to-follow steps. Photographs and line drawings are included to help clarify steps that are more difficult to explain or to master.

This book is geared toward the novice in the field of home improvements. It is assumed that the typical reader is the weekend or spare time home improver, and all language and terms are presented, when possible, in layman's language. When it is necessary to use more technical terms, these will be explained in the text or in the glossary. A detailed index and a table of contents will make it easier to locate specific instructions or descriptions of materials.

Most beginners will find that they will work very slowly at the beginning. This is not cause for discouragement. As familiarity and experience increase, speed will increase correspondingly.

A word of advice: let the job be a pleasure; learn to enjoy what you are doing. Siding installation can be a family affair, with duties for nearly all ages. Make the work a memorable and worthwhile experience. You'll be glad you did.

Chapter **1**

Sheathing

You cannot install any form of siding over just the framed walls with no form of buffer between siding and framing. The buffer material that separates exterior wall covering and the frame of the house is called *sheathing*.

TYPES OF SHEATHING

Sheathing, usually pronounced sheeting, can be diagonal boards, horizontal or vertical boards, oriented stress boards (OSB), rigid foam, traditional plywood, or so-called blackboard. The type of material used is largely a matter of personal choice, economy, and the time allotted for installation.

Diagonal board

Diagonal boards are superior in terms of strength, degree of insulation, and holding power. The boards, usually 1-×-5 or 1-×-4 units, are nailed from the lower corner of one wall to the upper corner of the same wall. If the boards are not long enough to reach the entire distance, other boards are butted end-to-end against the first pieces.

When installing diagonal board sheathing, measure the distance from the top corner on one wall to the bottom corner on the opposite wall and then fit your first boards from corner to corner. Use chalk lines to help guide your work. See FIG. 1-1.

Horizontal or vertical board

The disadvantages of horizontal sheathing boards are the cost and the installation—each board has to be nailed at every point where it crosses a corner post or stud or window or door frame. In addition to the cost of

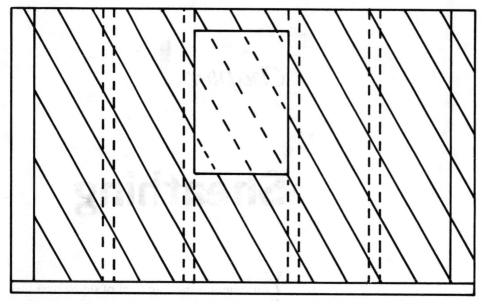

1-1   When placing chalking lines, mark across window openings and follow the line guides, but do not nail boards across openings.

the nails and the time needed for sawing, many nails are needed, and the time required to drive them is considerable.

Vertical boards and horizontal boards have the same drawbacks. The nailing time is essentially the same and the cost of the lumber remains unchanged. The major differences are that vertical or horizontal boards lack the strength, or holding power, of the diagonal manner of installation.

Oriented strand board

Oriented strand board (OSB) is a popular type of subflooring, and it is sometimes used as sheathing. It is strong, resists warping well, holds nails adequately (if grooved nails are used), and it can be installed quickly. Some builders complain that OSB tends to chip when nails are driven too close to the edges, but this problem can be solved by starting the nails an inch or so from the edge and slanting them slightly to hit the framing timbers well.

Waferboard

Waferboard, in the same family as OSB, is also used by many builders. It is easily handled and can be installed quickly, particularly if you have help, but like OSB, it has the slightly negative quality of chipping badly when you are sawing it. Be sure to use eye protection and gloves when you are handling any of the pressed wood or layered wood types of sheathing.

Plywood

Ordinary plywood is a superior form of sheathing. It provides excellent insulation and strength. When installed at the corners, it keeps the structure from warping or giving under stress. See FIG. 1-2.

1-2 Plywood panels used as corner bracing assures strong, square corners.

Rigid foam

Rigid foam sheathing is very easy to work with, cuts with no trouble, and does not have the disadvantage of extreme weight to be lifted and held in place. Some builders insist that the lack of strength is a negative characteristic while others point out that if plywood corners are installed, the rigid foam will work as well as any other type of sheathing. See FIG. 1-3.

Blackboard

Blackboard sheathing is heavier than rigid foam and is useless when it gets soaking wet, at which time it crumbles like cardboard. Wetting does not damage it when it is installed on the structure framing, but you cannot afford to allow it to lie on the wet ground or where it can absorb moisture.

Like many foam or particle products, blackboard sheathing breaks easily and offers too little strength or warp resistance to suit many workers. You can avoid the problem by using rigid foam or blackboard everywhere but corners. Then install plywood panels on both sides of all corners.

1-3 Rigid foam sheathing is light, easy to handle, easy to cut, and easy to install.

Some do-it-yourselfers prefer to use plywood for all sheathing purposes. The cost might run slightly higher than foam or blackboard sheathing, but plywood does not break, even under great stress, and it holds nails very well.

Plywood, which is composed of thin layers of wood glued and pressed so that alternate layers cross each other, is so strong that it can be used for aligning warped timbers or sagging joists. If a joist sags badly (or drops in the center an inch or more, even up to 4 or 5 inches), you can correct the sag by pushing the joist into proper position and then nailing a strip of plywood the same size as the joist along the side of the joist. Use a 4-foot strip on each side, and when the support is removed from under the joist, the timber will not sag.

This point is mentioned only to demonstrate the amazing strength of the material. When you install plywood, you can rest assured that the wall will not warp or give in any direction. Because the plywood is layered alternately, it has no grain, and therefore, no one spot or area will be weaker than the rest of the panel. Unlike grained wood, which might be strong in one direction but astonishingly weak in the other direction, the panel will hold in all directions.

A 12-inch board, for instance, possesses great strength along its length, but from side to side, it can be split by a sharp blow or from sudden or steady stress. Short sections of wide boards can be split simply by pushing on the unsupported center areas, but plywood resists breaking or splitting. You cannot split it even with an axe.

There are many trade names that combine many of the major advantages of plywood and foam insulation. Check with your dealer or ask professional builders about the products that offer the greatest strength, insulation, stress-resistance, and economy. You can write to manufacturers, but the obvious result is that each product will receive unqualified endorsement from its manufacturer. When you ask dealers for recommendations, ask about the R rating of the sheathing. An R rating is a value that indicates the total resistance of a material to allow heat to pass through. Another useful measurement is the U value. The U value is the amount of heat in British thermal units passing through 1 square foot of surface in one hour relative to each degree of difference between interior and exterior temperatures. Compare the rating with that of other products. The R value of 1 inch of wood, for example, is said to be 1.25, compared to the same thicknesses of cinder blocks (0.97), common bricks (0.20), face brick (0.11), or steel (0.0032). Learn as much as you can about the holding power of the product.

Is a product easily punctured? Is it likely to be damaged while you are hauling it? Does it resist wind pressure well? Is it fire-resistant? When exposed to excessive heat or fire, does the product emit poisonous fumes? These are questions that need to be answered.

If a product is easily damaged, you must think in terms of how many panels will be ruined while you are in the process of installing them. If the panels break when you walk on them or drop a timber on them, you need to consider how safely you can store the sheathing until you are ready to use it.

Do not settle for the first product the dealer shows you. He may have a special price in effect, but on the other hand, he might need to move outdated materials. Research the materials available and get the best buy for your money.

You can purchase products that have very high R-ratings, are not flammable, do not emit toxic fumes, possess great strength, will not warp or split, and are not unduly heavy. You must also consider the cost.

You also need to consider whether the sheathing material can be cut with a knife or whether it will require a power tool. Is it lightweight enough so that it can be handled easily by one person of average or little strength? How will the sheathing be applied to the framing? You can nail or staple some sheathing panels, and you can buy these products in a wide variety of thicknesses or grades.

WRAPPING THE HOUSE

With all building projects, consult your local building inspector's office before you move too rapidly. Ask whether you must wrap the house during the installation processes before sheathing is installed. Most inspectors are willing and even anxious to answer your questions before you start to work.

Remember that the building code in your area does not represent the highest level of building. Contrary, it is the *lowest* permissible standard. The building inspector's job is to see that you do not engage in a building practice that will result in a personal danger or weaknesses that will result in loss of integrity of the building materials. The inspector is not your enemy. He is there to help you, and it is in your best interest to work with him and comply with all standards.

If the inspector tells you that the house must be wrapped, then make your plans accordingly. Wrapping keeps air from infiltrating and causing heating or cooling loss. Some products are designed to be used over sheathing so that no wind can penetrate the exterior siding and into the sheathing. See FIGS. 1-4 and 1-5.

I-4 Stretch building wrap tightly across the wall framing and secure it to prevent sagging or tearing.

I-5 Stretch building wrap around corners and fasten securely for a neat and effective job.

Some wrapping is applied directly to the studs rather than to the sheathing. When you decide to use wrapping, buy a clear wrap so that you can see the studs easily. You can also buy a special tape to use when sealing doors and windows.

Remember that when you seal the house against wind, you will be saving on heating and cooling for the life of the house. When you install wrapping, start near a corner. Allow the wrap to reach 2 or 3 feet around the corner and then fasten the end. Use plenty of staples or nails (with large heads) or glue.

Pull the wrapping around the corner and start down the length of the exterior wall framing. Do not cut out for windows, doors, or any other openings. The wrapping can be cut away from openings with a knife. Use tape to seal windows and doors. See FIG. 1-6. When you complete one section and prepare to start another, be sure to lap the second wrapping over the top edge of the first by 2 to 3 inches.

1-6 Much of the heating and cooling loss around windows and doors can be eliminated with building wrap.

Measure the width of the wrapping and compare this to the length of the house wall from top to bottom of the framing. If you see that the wrapping widths will allow several inches too much for the height of the wall, divide the number of the excess inches and let that be your lap amount.

Suppose that you will need three strands of wrapping and you will have 9 inches left over. Use a 3-inch lap to use the excess. If you have 12 inches too much, use a 4-inch lap. Do not try to cut corners by lapping too little. This only allows for wind and heat loss.

You should also investigate the need for vapor barriers inside the walls. If the wall is near the kitchen, bathroom, or laundry room, you will have a great deal of moisture in the rooms and you might need the vapor barrier. Check the building codes in your area. Some codes will not permit two barriers. In this case, you can omit the vapor barrier. See FIG. 1-7.

Ask your dealer or factory representative about the ratings of the vapor barriers. Learn what the thicknesses are, how rapidly they allow

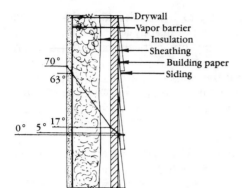

1-7 A typical wall structure, with interior drywall covering, vapor barrier to prevent excessive moisture from entering, insulation to cut heating and cooling loss, sheathing over the insulation, building paper, and finally, the siding.

cold or heat to penetrate, and how you can create the maximum savings in heat or cooling at the best installation prices. Compare literature on various products.

Remember that insulation cannot prevent heat and cold from passing through a wall. The role of insulation is to slow down the passage of cold or heat as much as possible. A wall that has the absurd amount of 60 inches of insulation will allow cold to pass all the way through, eventually, but the time required is of the utmost importance.

In the same sense, insulation of 6 inches will not allow heat or cold loss as rapidly as will insulation layers of only 3 inches. Remember that the dead air space in the wall is extremely valuable in preventing passage of heat and cold.

When you use a foam type of sheathing and cover the windows, you can go inside the house and use a sharp knife with a long blade and cut along the inside edge of the window framing. Make the cut all the way around the window and the sheathing foam will fall out. You can then save the section to use for smaller areas such as those over door framing.

INSTALLING SHEATHING PANELS

If you choose to install plywood, OSB, waferboard, or similar products, you will find that these panels weigh several times as much as foam panels. You will also find it difficult to carry, lift, position, and hold the panels in place while you nail. If you are working alone, there are several techniques that will help you to install these heavy panels. The first device is to drive two or three nails into the crevice where the foundation wall meets the joists. Space the nails so that they are spread well over a 4-foot section of horizontal space.

When you are working at a corner, drive two or three nails into the corner post around the corner from the wall you are sheathing. Drive one nail two feet from the top of the foundation wall, the second at the 4-foot height, and the third at 6 feet.

Start the nails an inch or so from the corner of the corner post and when they are driven in sufficiently to hold weight against them, bend the nails so that they stick past the actual corner an inch or so. The nails can then be used to hold the panel of plywood in place later. See FIG. 1-8.

When nails are in place at the corner and the meeting point where the wall frame and foundation wall meet, lift the plywood and set the bottom edge upon the nails at the foundation wall. With the panel resting in place, shift it so that the outside edge is flush against the nails in the corner post.

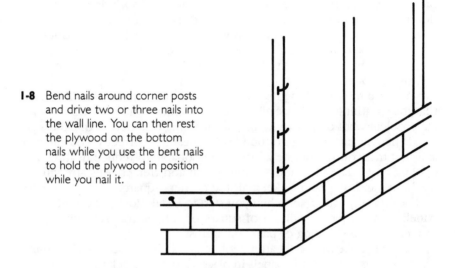

1-8 Bend nails around corner posts and drive two or three nails into the wall line. You can then rest the plywood on the bottom nails while you use the bent nails to hold the plywood in position while you nail it.

Lean against the panel to hold it in place and start several nails. Double-check to see that the panel is still in place, and then drive the nails into the studs or the corner post. Two or three nails will hold the panel in place so you can back away to look to see if the position is correct. Do not drive the nails in all the way. Sink them sufficiently to hold the panel securely in place.

If all is correct, continue to nail the plywood, OSB, or particleboard in place. If the edge of the panel does not conform exactly with the edge of the corner post, pull the nails out enough to free the panel and readjust. Try again, and when the panel is in the perfect position, finish nailing the plywood to the wall framing.

You should use plenty of nails in each panel. Space them a foot or so apart on every corner post, partition stud, or common stud. Do not try to economize by using too few nails.

For the next panel, you need to use only the nails at the juncture of the foundation wall and the bottom of the foundation timbers. Rest the panel on the nails, position, then drive the nails the rest of the way in.

If your studs are spaced exactly as they should be—16 inches on center—you can start several nails in the upper part of the panel even before you lift it into position. Do not start nails in the middle or bottom part.

You will be carrying the panel and the lower nails will possibly scratch you painfully.

For best results, use full panels installed vertically. You can cut other panels lengthwise to use over the vertical panels. Cut out for windows and other wall irregularities. If your studs are not spaced correctly, you might need to mark the location of the studs by making a pencil mark at the top and bottom of the panel so that you will know where to nail.

When you have installed all of the whole pieces that can be used, go back and use partial pieces to fill in over and under windows and over doors. You can cut a panel lengthwise and use the two halves to install over vertical panels. Each long strip will cover two full vertical panels.

Do not be concerned if some of your panels do not fit together precisely. Remember that the studs will prevent air passage and subsequent loss of heat or cooling.

You can mix sheathing materials without undue problems. Take care that the sheathing panels are all the same thickness and you will not create problems, but do not try to install sheathing of different thicknesses.

When the entire house or building is sheathed correctly, you can rest satisfied that you have done all that is reasonable to reduce heating and cooling costs. The plywood sheathing will add tremendous strength to the house and will help to keep all the corners square. This squareness will be crucially important when you start to install siding or even indoor paneling. A corner or wall out of square of vertical trueness will be extremely hard to fit siding or paneling against.

Before you leave the sheathing job, make a visual check to determine that you have nailed all the panels in place securely. Check to see that you have used enough nails in the studding and posts.

When you are assured that the job is completed to your satisfaction, you are ready to start on installing the siding itself. Remember, once you leave the sheathing, you cannot return to make corrections without going to a great deal of trouble. You will need to remove the siding in order to reach the sheathing. If you install brick siding, it will be a major undertaking to remove the work, not to mention the cost and time expended.

CHOOSING SIDING

When you are ready to install siding, your choices are many, each with disadvantages and advantages. Some require great skill in installation while some can be handled with ease by the novice do-it-yourselfer.

Masonry work is generally more difficult than wood or vinyl materials. Spend some time determining what you want to use; don't be led into quick decisions.

Vinyl or aluminum sidings can be installed quickly in the sense that you can cover many square feet simply by driving a few nails, once your preliminary work is done. Masonry work moves very slowly for the beginner. Shakes and shingles are fairly easy to install satisfactorily.

Do not let difficulty of the job prevent you from choosing the siding that will suit you best. If you want and need bricks, learn to install them.

Rather than be intimidated by the job, remember that every expert mason or siding technician was, at one point, as intimidated as you might be.

You might, in fact, wish to use several different types of sidings on your house. You might want to use bricks for the basic walls and then vinyl siding for the eaves, soffit, fascia, and perhaps aluminum for window and door moldings. Many houses incorporate combinations of shingles and shakes, bricks, and vinyl.

Remember that you also have log sidings to choose from. These units can create a beautiful exterior for your house. They are fairly easy to install and you need no special equipment or machinery.

Part of your choice might be affected by the area in which you live. If your house is in the country where houses are wide apart, nearly any form of siding will be in place. If you live in an urban development you may want to consider the types of siding used on the other houses around you and then decide whether the siding of your choice will blend well with the houses in closest proximity.

The architecture of your house will also play an important part in your choice. Ask your dealer to show you some photos of houses similar to yours and study the visual effect of bricks, vinyl, shakes and shingles, and other types of sidings.

When you have determined what looks best and is most economical, seek help in buying. Many salespersons will tell you if the materials will be on sale in the near future. You might find that buying all of the materials at once will result in a better unit price, just be sure that you can store the materials safely at your construction site. Vandals and thieves can eliminate economy quickly by ruining or hauling off your property.

Chapter 2 covers siding with brick. Laying bricks is not an easy task, but neither is it so hard that you can't learn to do it. A quick review of chapter 2 can help you decide whether you are willing to undertake the job.

Chapter 2

Brick siding

*B*ricks are among the oldest building materials known to man. Although immense trees were once readily available, men in earlier civilizations lacked the equipment to cut the timbers properly and efficiently. They also lacked the innovative skills to fashion saws from metal. What they did know, however, was how to manipulate the earth to make bricks, so virtually all construction work was done by masonry.

There were other reasons for brick's immense popularity: they do not burn; they are reasonably good insulation materials; they do not decay; they are not subject to insect attack; and they were available virtually everywhere in Europe.

Brick buildings have been around for at least 5,000 years, and it is difficult to tell the difference between a brick wall only a year old and one that is two centuries old. See FIG. 2-1. Bricks are highly attractive, very durable, and most important, nearly maintenance-free. While a wood house must be repainted every five years or so, bricks retain their original color and never need painting. You save on the cost of hiring a painter or buying your own ladders and scaffolding as well as brushes, rollers, and perhaps sprayers.

There is an astonishing array of brick styles, shapes, and colors to choose from. In fact, there are an estimated 10,000 possible brick choices. Figure 2-2 shows a sampling of just some of these various brick sizes and shapes. Although you can buy bricks in a number of sizes and weights, the typical brick is 4 inches thick, 8 inches long, and 2¼ inches high.

Brick color is determined by the clay used in making the brick. The color extends throughout the entire brick. See FIG. 2-3. If you were to break a brick, you would see that the color in the center is the same as that of the exterior surface.

If time is not a factor, I would suggest that you enroll in a bricklaying

2-1 This house was built about the time of the American Revolution, and the bricks are still sturdy, strong, and attractive.

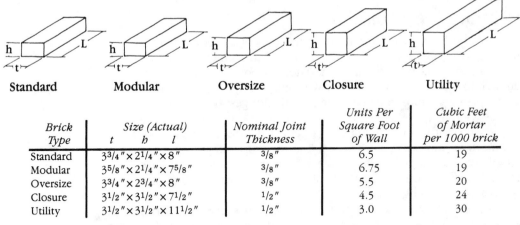

| Standard | Modular | Oversize | Closure | Utility |

Brick Type	Size (Actual) t h l	Nominal Joint Thickness	Units Per Square Foot of Wall	Cubic Feet of Mortar per 1000 brick
Standard	3³/₄″ × 2¹/₄″ × 8″	3/8″	6.5	19
Modular	3⁵/₈″ × 2¹/₄″ × 7⁵/₈″	3/8″	6.75	19
Oversize	3³/₄″ × 2³/₄″ × 8″	3/8″	5.5	20
Closure	3¹/₂″ × 3¹/₂″ × 7¹/₂″	1/2″	4.5	24
Utility	3¹/₂″ × 3¹/₂″ × 11¹/₂″	1/2″	3.0	30

2-2 Several sizes and types of bricks. Note the variety of sizes and also the amount of mortar needed and the number of bricks needed for a square foot of wall space.

class in time to study the art before you start to work. Many high schools teach the course as part of their vocational curriculum, and technical institutes and community colleges often include bricklaying as part of their course offerings.

If you want to have brick siding but lack the courage to take on the job, one possible alternative is to hire a part-time mason and work as his helper. This way, you can learn the trade while watching the professional

2-3 Bricks are available in a wide range of colors and hues. Choose the color of brick that will best fit the design of your house.

at work. You can also secure the materials you want and make your own plans.

MATERIALS AND EQUIPMENT

Keep in mind that you can rent many of the tools and equipment needed for bricklaying if you don't want to make the investment. Your first need is for a mixing box or mortar pan. There are metal pans that are deep enough to mix a full bag of mortar without having it slop over the edges. These pans are almost 5 feet in length (at the longest point) and about 30-inches wide.

An alternative to a mixing box is a construction wheelbarrow. When the mortar is mixed, you can wheel it to the work site without having to handle the mortar twice. When the wheelbarrow is not being used as a mortar box, you can use it for hauling other materials, such as bricks, sand, gravel, cement, or concrete blocks.

You will also need a good trowel, a carpenter's level, measuring tape, hoe, shovel, line level, framing square, and masonry hammer. A good nylon or similar mason's line will also be needed.

Select a trowel that feels good to your hand. Hold it so that your fingers curve around the handle and your thumb lies along the handle and pointed directly at the point of the trowel. The trowel should be made of metal thick enough to hold a good load of mortar without bending or sagging. You will use the trowel for several purposes, so don't try to save money by buying the cheapest one available.

Your best bet for a level is a carpenter's level at least 3- or 4-feet long. Shorter levels will work but it is more difficult to see the lack of trueness in a level or vertical reading taken over a short distance. The drawback is that 4-foot levels cost at least three to five times as much as shorter ones.

The measuring tape should be 16 to 25-feet long and should be made of good metal so that it will not bend when you extend it several feet. A regular garden hoe will suffice for mixing mortar but the masonry hoe has holes in it to allow the mixture to pass through. The latter hoe makes the work much easier but is not totally necessary, and you can always use a garden hoe for gardening after the masonry work is done.

The shovel should have a strong handle so that you can lift a full load of gravel, mortar, or concrete. The least expensive line level you can find will work about as well as the most expensive. Your greatest concern is the ability to see the bubble clearly.

You can buy smaller squares, such as the quick-square, but for masonry work, you need a good 2-foot square with clearly marked gradations. You will use the square very frequently, so buy one that is sturdy and durable enough to last.

A cement or mortar mixer is a highly desirable item to have, but these cost a great deal of money, and if you are planning to do only one large masonry job, you could be able to pay a mason for several hours with what the mixer would cost you. You can rent mixers, but most companies charge by the day, and you will need the mixer for weeks, not days, unless you are able to work faster than most amateurs. The rental cost would pay a considerable portion of the cost of buying the mixer.

If you don't want to buy or rent a mixer, you can mix the mortar and concrete by hand. The work is slower than using a mixer and the work is hard, but you can do it if you want to save the money.

You will also need sand, water, gravel, and Portland cement for making concrete and mortar. Other items that you might need when working with bricks and mortar are a brick or masonry chisel, wall ties, metal lintels, a stiff-bristled brush, and a jointer.

A special word of caution is in order here about cement. When mortar or cement is exposed to dampness for a period of weeks, moisture penetrates the bags and causes the mix to set up. There might not be huge lumps; maybe the size of a marble only, but these will not break down and mix into mortar. You cannot lay bricks with these lumps in the mortar, so you must either painstakingly remove the lumps, or discard the entire box of mortar as well as all the other bags that are lumpy.

When you buy mortar mix, beware of firms that offer the bags on sale for unusually low prices. Often, these bags have been exposed to excessive dampness and cannot be used for laying bricks or blocks. Pay the full price, if necessary, and buy first-class mortar. The few dollars you save will be lost instantly in wasted mortar and the time needed to pick the lumps out.

You might discover that you need other small tools, but these are available at any hardware dealer's and can be bought for a very small price. You might already have some of them on hand, so don't plan to buy them until you see whether you will need them.

POURING FOOTINGS

You probably had footings poured when the foundation walls for the house were constructed. Generally, the footings are wide enough for foundation walls as well as brick siding. You will need slightly more than 4 inches of footings. You might have to dig to find the footings and possibly excavate them so you can work easily and comfortably in the space available.

If the footings are not adequate and you need to pour a wider footing, you must dig through the topsoil until you reach the hard, packed clay. Keep in mind that you will be laying several courses of bricks on top of the footing, which must be strong and stable enough to hold the weight of about 36 bricks—one on top of the other.

Before you are ready to pour footings, you must set up stakes to indicate the concrete level. The concrete footings should be as level as possible from one corner of the house to the next around the entire house. If the footings are not level, you'll wind up with a discrepancy at the end of the first brick course, and the result will be bricks that continue to drift uphill or downhill, resulting in a very unsightly appearance. Such a discrepancy will be particularly noticeable under windows and above them.

Often, footings are dug along the foundation wall lines and are only shallow trenches below the grade line of the basement or ground surface. The concrete is then poured in the trenches to the specified level. If the house is on a steep slope, forms might be built of plywood or other wide boards. The concrete is then poured into the existing trench (if any) and brought up to the desired level on the forms.

To achieve a proper footing level, drive a stake into the ground past the end of the footing. Drive another at the other end. Then stretch a good line from one stake to the other and at the center of the line hang the line level. Raise or lower the line at one end until the level is perfect.

Standing in front of the house, let the corner to your left be Corner A; the one to your right Corner B. The one behind Corner A will be C, and the one behind B will be D. When you have a perfect level from Corner A to B, drive stakes past the end of the footing at points C and D. Use the line level to determine the proper level by raising or lowering the line at Corner C only or Corner D only. Do not change the level where you first worked, between Corner A and B.

When the line is level from A to C, then level the line from B to D. The line from C to D should now be perfectly level. While the line is in place, drive small wood stakes at several points between Corners A and B, etc. Mark the stakes at the right level or drive them deep enough into the ground so that the top of the stake is perfectly level with the line. Do this on all four lines. Be sure that the string or line is pulled tight between stakes at all times. Do not allow the line to sag.

Mixing mortar

Once footings are level, you can begin the concrete work. If you are working alone or without a mixer, you might want to mix only half a bag of concrete at a time. You will need sand, water, gravel, and Portland cement. The proper mix is 1:3:5. What this means is: for every shovelful of cement, you will need three shovelfuls of sand and five shovelfuls of gravel. The sand is often called the fine aggregate and the gravel is the coarse aggregate.

Masons disagree on the best methods of mixing. One easy way is to start with half the water you expect to need. Then add half the sand for that batch and mix thoroughly. Do not simply wet the sand. Saturate it. Add more water and more sand, if necessary, until the sand and water mix is complete. Then add the cement, five or six shovelfuls at a time, until you have a soupy mixture.

Now add gravel, half a dozen shovelfuls at a time, until all the gravel is mixed thoroughly with the other ingredients. For half a bag of cement, you will probably need 3 gallons or slightly more of water, 12 shovelfuls of sand, and 16 shovelfuls of gravel. Keep the moisture level high enough that you can work the mix easily. Don't let it become too stiff.

When you are ready, dump the concrete into the footing trench and spread it evenly so that the top of the concrete mix is even with the top of the stakes. Use a trowel or float to spread the concrete. Take out all ridges and humps, and use your level regularly to see that you are staying level from one point to the next.

Continue the process around the house until the footings are completed. Let the footings set for several hours, preferably overnight, before you begin to lay bricks.

SELECTING BOND AND JOINT METHODS

You can create a bond by laying bricks in a particular arrangement. There are five basic bond patterns or methods: the running bond, common bond, Flemish bond, English bond, and stack bond. Take a look at FIG. 2-4 to familiarize yourself with the positions of bricks in a wall.

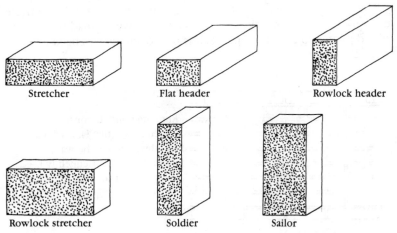

2-4 The six basic brick positions in a typical wall. The stretcher is the most common position.

The running bond

The running bond consists of all "stretchers," or bricks laid end to end lengthwise along a course in a building project. Each stretcher brick ends halfway across the brick below it.

The common bond

The common bond method is very similar to the running bond. The major difference is that the common bond method includes a row of headers every five or six, even seven, courses. The header bricks are only ordinary bricks laid crosswise in the course so that the ends of the bricks are visible from outside the structure.

The Flemish bond

Flemish bond is made up of stretchers and headers, one beside the other, throughout courses. In each course, is a stretcher, then a header, then another stretcher, then another header, etc. The headers are centered over the stretchers in all cases.

The English bond

The English bond is somewhat similar. There are alternating courses of headers and stretchers, with headers centered over stretchers and all joints between stretchers lined up vertically.

Stack bonding

Stack bonding means that the courses will consist of either all headers or all stretchers and with all vertical joints lined up. As the name implies, you simply stack one brick on top of another and mortar between bricks and at end joints. See FIG. 2-5.

The six basic types of joints are the concave, V-shaped, weathered, struck, rough cut, and raked joint. The concave is made by using a rounded jointer so that the joint itself is round and curves back under the edge of the brick.

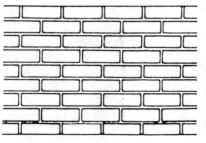

Running bond. It consists of all "stretchers" (that is, brick laid lengthwise along the wall). Running bond is frequently used in veneered walls and in interior walls.

2-5   The five basic types of bonds used in brick masonry.

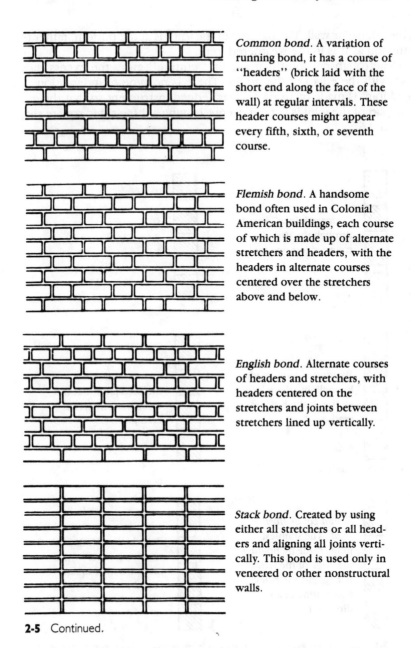

Common bond. A variation of running bond, it has a course of "headers" (brick laid with the short end along the face of the wall) at regular intervals. These header courses might appear every fifth, sixth, or seventh course.

Flemish bond. A handsome bond often used in Colonial American buildings, each course of which is made up of alternate stretchers and headers, with the headers in alternate courses centered over the stretchers above and below.

English bond. Alternate courses of headers and stretchers, with headers centered on the stretchers and joints between stretchers lined up vertically.

Stack bond. Created by using either all stretchers or all headers and aligning all joints vertically. This bond is used only in veneered or other nonstructural walls.

2-5 Continued.

The V-shaped joint can be created with an angled tool such as the edge of a brick or 2×4. The weathered joint is slanted from the bottom to the top so that the top is recessed a fraction of an inch. The effect is much like clapboard siding, which sheds water readily.

The struck joint is the exact opposite of the weathered joint. This joint slopes from the top to the bottom and the slant is toward the inside of the course or wall. The flat part of the joint is at the bottom, rather than at the top as it is in the weathered joint.

The rough cut joint is made by "cutting" away the excess mortar flush with the edges of the bricks. There is no type of indentation. The raked joint is made by using a square-edged instrument so that the entire front part of the joint is cut out evenly, leaving a three-sided square shape. See FIG. 2-6.

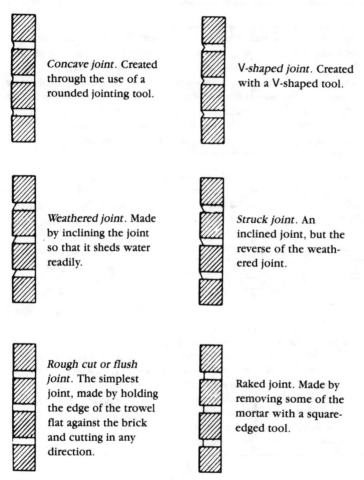

Concave joint. Created through the use of a rounded jointing tool.

V-shaped joint. Created with a V-shaped tool.

Weathered joint. Made by inclining the joint so that it sheds water readily.

Struck joint. An inclined joint, but the reverse of the weathered joint.

Rough cut or flush joint. The simplest joint, made by holding the edge of the trowel flat against the brick and cutting in any direction.

Raked joint. Made by removing some of the mortar with a square-edged tool.

2-6 Six joint types, with the concave joint perhaps the most common.

Arches and quoins are essential parts of masonry, but these techniques are usually handled by experienced brick masons. See FIGS. 2-7 and 2-8. The illustrations here show how the arches and quoins are constructed and how the bricks and joints are positioned in relation to each other. Beginning masons should practice on small projects before they

QUOIN CORNER

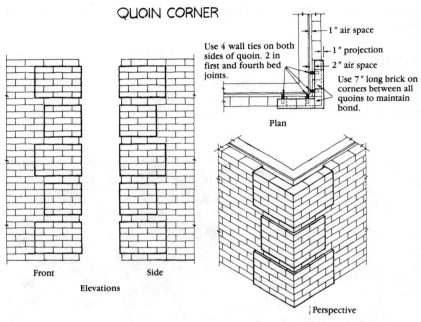

Use 4 wall ties on both sides of quoin. 2 in first and fourth bed joints.

1″ air space
1″ projection
2″ air space

Use 7″ long brick on corners between all quoins to maintain bond.

Plan

Front　Side

Elevations

Perspective

2-7 Special quoin corner masonry requires more skill than the typical beginner possesses, but you can study the illustration and practice the corners on small projects.

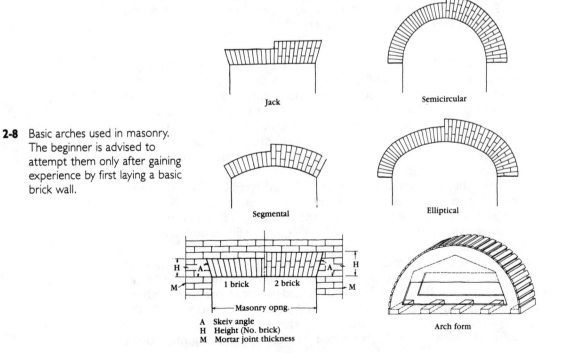

Jack

Semicircular

2-8 Basic arches used in masonry. The beginner is advised to attempt them only after gaining experience by first laying a basic brick wall.

Segmental

Elliptical

H
A
M
1 brick　2 brick
Masonry opng.

A　Skeiv angle
H　Height (No. brick)
M　Mortar joint thickness

Arch form

attempt to construct arch work on a large scale or in the interior of a house.

LAYING THE BRICKS

When footings are ready and the foundation wall is completed, you can start to lay bricks. Most builders lay a foundation wall of concrete blocks and then lay the bricks against the blocks. See FIG. 2-9.

2-9 After you have poured a solid footing and have it inspected, lay the foundation wall. Incorporate vents to prevent excessive dampness under the structure. You can now lay brick veneer siding when the house is framed.

Brick quality is usually very uniform, but no matter how much care is used in the manufacturing of the bricks, there will be slight differences in color or shade of color. Sometimes, this tiny variation adds to the attractiveness of the job, but if you have more than a trivial discrepancy, go through your bricks and sort them when you are nearing the end of the job. If some are noticeably darker, lay these apart. Do the same with lighter ones. Mix these so that they tend to blend in a uniform progression rather than in a glaringly obvious manner.

You might also want to use any radically different bricks in the most obscure locations, such as behind drains or where shrubbery will conceal the defects. Keep your best bricks for use in the upper part of the walls and particularly at eye-level heights where they are far more likely to be seen and noticed.

Once bricks are sorted, start by laying out a good supply of bricks at the first corner where you plan to work. If you have never laid bricks before, three important suggestions are in order: first, mix a small amount of mortar; second, plan to work very slowly; third, start to work in the least noticeable point, such as the back corners.

You will need to build corners first. Lay dry bricks along the footing from Corner C to Corner A. Leave a small space between bricks to allow for mortar. By dry-laying the bricks you can see whether the bricks will fit snugly into the space allocated. You will have to break or cut bricks in each course. See FIG. 2-10.

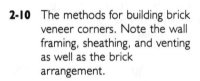
2-10 The methods for building brick veneer corners. Note the wall framing, sheathing, and venting as well as the brick arrangement.

Determine the exact corner point to start. Lay your square so that the two points extend along the walls of the house frame. Now, move the square out slightly until the tip of the point is 4 inches from the foundation wall. Use a pencil point to trace the outside lines of the square.

Now, mix your mortar if it isn't ready. Use the same formula you used for gravel, but omit the gravel. For one full bag of mortar mix, use 5 gallons of water and 22 shovelfuls of sand. Start by mixing water and sand, then add mortar mix. Mix thoroughly. Scrape the hoe blade along the bottom of the mortar box or wheelbarrow to see that there are no clumps of dry sand or mortar that did not mix well. If you are using a wheelbarrow for a mortar box, you should not mix more than half a bag of mortar mix. Cut the other two ingredients in half also.

Lay a bed of mortar with the trowel along the lines you made with the pencil. Extend the mortar bed from the outside line to the foundation wall and at least 3 feet in each direction.

Lay the first brick so that the end of the brick is perfectly even with the line of the foundation wall. Use the square to see that the alignment is perfect. Press the brick into the mortar with gentle and even pressure.

Force mortar into the holes in the brick. Much of the holding power of the mortar is derived from the holes.

Lay another brick at a right angle to the first one so that the end of the second brick is perfectly even with the outside edge of the first brick. Push this brick into the mortar as you did the first one.

Use your carpenter's level to ensure that the two bricks are level, both with each other and from end to end. You can lay several bricks along the two lines now. Lay five bricks in each direction, first laying a good bed of mortar and then pushing the bricks gently into the bed. Use the level to ensure a true line.

You will need to "butter" each brick after the first one. If you are right-handed, hold the brick across the top so that the fingers of your left hand are on one side and your thumb on the other. Turn the brick slightly upward so that the end of the brick is in a ten o'clock position. With your right hand, dip the trowel into the mortar and spread a small amount of mortar across the ends of the brick from top to bottom. Push the brick against the first brick so that the mortar is slightly compressed and then press the brick into the mortar bed. Check the level of the two bricks with a carpenter's level or a masonry level.

After you have laid five bricks in one direction, lay five more in the other direction. Go back to the corner where you laid the first brick and lay a mortar bed across the tops of the bricks you have just laid.

Start the second course of the corner by laying the first brick so that the end of the brick is aligned perfectly with the outside edge of the first brick laid. You have, when this is done, completed the first bond. If properly laid, the last brick laid reached across the first brick so that half of the first brick is covered by the first brick in the second course.

The brick just laid will end halfway across the second brick in the first course. A second bond is then established. Continue to lay bricks fo the course until you reach the end of the first five bricks. Do this on both sides of the corner. At the end of each course or line of bricks, you'll have half a brick left over, provided you achieved a correct bonding pattern.

You should never have the brick in one course end where the brick immediately below it ended. If you do, you do not have a bond and the wall will not be secure. Bonding holds the bricks in place.

You can continue to build short courses until you reach the top of the fifth course. At this point, you will not have any more room to lay bricks because you have decreased the length of the course line by half a brick with each course.

Use the level frequently both to check the level of the course line and for true vertical reading. Hold the level against the sides of the bricks to see if you are plumb, and hold it diagonally to see that your bonding is holding true.

Now move to the other corner, which is D. Build another corner there, and use the line level to be sure that the top of the first brick in the new corner is perfectly level with the top of the first brick in the first corner.

If the second corner is slightly lower then the first, make the mortar bed slightly thicker until the discrepancy is corrected. If it is too high, then make the mortar bed slightly thinner.

There is a very good reason for using the line level. It keeps you on the correct level. If the line is even with the tops of the bricks at the corner, then the tops of the bricks you lay ought to be even with the line also.

When the second corner is built, you will have two good corners and short course lines starting toward the other two corners. If all is going well, move next to Corners A and B and repeat the process. When these corners are started, you should have four perfectly level corners five courses high.

At this time, you can start to lay the bricks between the four corners. Start at any wall you prefer and stretch a line all the way from the top of the first brick in each corner. Lay the bricks between the two points, taking care to see that the top of each brick is level with the line.

You can complete the wall between the two corners, and then do the same with the other three walls. Or you can build your corners all the way to the top of the wall if you prefer. This way, you can rest assured that you are progressing accurately. You can, if you build the corners all the way to the top of the wall, complete one wall at a time, completing the entire structure in this fashion.

Use plenty of wall ties along the wall. These are thin metal strips that are nailed to the sheathing or to the studding and then are bent so that the strip, which is serrated, lies across the course of bricks. The strip is embedded in the mortar and when the mortar dries, the wall is strongly supported.

CUTTING BRICKS

In alternating courses, you might need to break or cut a brick for a perfect fit. Because of the bonding pattern, your bricks should always end halfway across the top of the brick below it, so there will be a point where half a brick might be needed.

Use a brick or masonry chisel to cut a brick. Set the chisel in the center of the brick and tap the end of the chisel with a hammer. Move the chisel blade after each tap until the brick top is scored all the way across.

Bricks have "grains" of sorts. While not like wood grains, the molecular structure of the brick is such that the brick, when scored, will break cleanly and straight. When the scoring is done, place the blade of the chisel in the center of the brick and strike the end of the chisel sharply with a hammer. The brick should easily snap in half.

You can also hold the brick across the palm of your hand and strike the brick across the edge with a brick or masonry hammer and the brick will, after two or three blows, break in half.

If, during delivery, several bricks were broken, you can use these partials to fill out a course. You can also saw the bricks with a special blade for a circular saw, but the dust is extremely bad and there is a danger of flying chips. If you saw bricks, use eye protection and glasses.

WINDOWS AND DOORS

When you reach windows and doors, you will continue to lay bricks as you did before. Because these areas are so much more conspicuous than the middle portions of the wall, you will want to use the greatest care to see that your work is neat and that the bricks are the most attractive you have.

Installing lintels

You will need to install lintels over doorways and windows and any other interruptions in the wall line. The reason is simple: there will be nothing to support the bricks in the expanse over the doors and windows.

A lintel usually consists of a length of metal that is laid into the mortar bed on each side of the window or door. The metal length stretches across the opening and is mortared in place. It is usually about the thickness of the mortar joint and not quite as wide. You can spread a small amount of mortar into the joint to cover the metal. You might need to thicken the mortar bed slightly if the lintel is too thick for the regular mortar joints.

To install the lintels, spread the mortar bed as you would for bricks, and then push the ends of the lintel into the mortar bed. When you reach the lintel, spread mortar across the lintel just as you would if it were a brick course. Then lay the bricks across the metal. The thickness and corresponding strength of the metal will support the weight of the bricks above it. See FIG. 2-11.

2-11 When a lentil is installed over a door or window, you might need to support the work until the mortar sets. This 2 × 4 will be left overnight before it is removed.

JOINTING

After you have worked for an hour or so, you need to stop and joint the bricks you have laid. This means compressing the mortar joints so that they tighten and seal better.

You can joint by using a wide variety of tools. The simplest device is the tip of your finger, although in the course of a lot of work, the process can be painful.

The simplest and handiest device is the corner of a brick. Hold the brick so that the corner of one end will reach slightly into the mortar joint. Start at the top of the joint and rake the end of the brick downward so the mortar inside the joint is pushed against the sides of the joint. You can also use a short length of 2×4 in the same manner. There are jointers you can buy, particularly if you want a special effect, however.

Do not let the mortar harden or set before you begin to joint. Stop every half hour or so and joint the work you have completed, except for the most recent work that is still too plastic.

FINISHING UP

At the end of each day's work, there are several crucial tasks that must be done. One of the most important of these is brushing the bricks you have laid. As you worked, you undoubtedly spilled small amounts of mortar, and this mortar will stick to the bricks and dry there. Once it has set fully, it is very difficult to remove. So before it is completely set, brush the mortar crumbs off with a stiff-bristled brush or with a broom.

Another job is that of washing any discolorations that have occurred. Do not spray a hose on fresh mortar work, but if some bricks have been stained during the work, you can take a damp cloth, preferably a rough one, and clean the bricks easily by swabbing at the spots until they come clean.

When excessive mortar has been pushed out of the bed, you should "cut" away the mortar by turning the trowel so that it is flat against the wall and swing it sharply. The trowel edge will cut away all superfluous mortar and leave neat joints.

Be sure to cover your bricks at the end of a day's work. Rain will not harm the bricks but soaking wet bricks are hard to lay. It is also a good idea to cover sand with a section of plastic. Wet sand can be difficult to work with, particularly in cold weather. The moisture in the sand freezes and causes the sand to form hard lumps. By all means cover the cement and mortar mix. Once these items become wet, they start to set up and cannot be used.

If bricklaying is not for you, perhaps you might be interested in the many wood sidings, which are covered in detail in chapter 3.

Chapter **3**

Wood siding

*T*here are several types of wood siding, including plywood, particleboard, and hardboard. Wood panels for exterior siding are manufactured in a variety of ways. Plywood is a cross laminated wood veneer, composites are veneer face bonded to reconstituted wood cores, and the non-veneered panels include waferboard, oriented strand board (OSB), and certain classes of particleboard. There is a wide range of thicknesses, grades, and designs. Product and performance standards vary considerably also. Larger lumberyards and home centers have wide selections.

Most hardboard siding is made from processed wood, binders, and overlays. The composites are manufactured by several material corporations, offering a variety in materials.

According to recent studies, hardboard accounts for 19.2 percent of all siding sales with plywood at 7.9 percent. The most popular siding materials are: stucco, 22.5 percent; brick, 19.5 percent; hardboard, 19.2 percent; vinyl, 12.4 percent; plywood, 7.9 percent; aluminum, 3.0 percent; shakes and shingles, 1.7 percent; and others, 13.2 percent.

REDWOOD

Redwood siding is attractive and permits weather-tight joints. U.S. Forestry laboratory tests have shown that no other wood exhibits less shrinkage than redwood.

Certified kiln dried redwood has been preshrunk for the best possible performance. Because redwood shrinks less, it is less likely to warp, cup, or check. It also tends to hold paints, stains, and finishes better than other woods. Its very light wood also requires little maintenance.

Properties of redwood

Redwood heartwood is decay and insect resistant, qualities not found in other natural and chemically treated woods. Unlike pressure-treated lumber, redwood heartwood is the same throughout, not just on the surface. Because it contains little or no pitch or resins and has a unique cellular structure it accepts finishes well.

Redwood texture and grain patterns make it highly workable. It can also be sawn, bored, nailed, and shaped with ease. It has great nail-holding power and pops fewer nails than most other woods. It has a strong resistance to disintegration when exposed to a wide range of chemical solutions and fumes at different temperatures. The durability of redwood has long been important in industrial applications, ranging from textiles to beverages, and has been used to construct cooling towers.

One of the lightest softwoods used for structural purposes, reportedly weighing only 28 pounds per cubic foot, redwood still has rather good strength. Some builders feel its insulation values are better than more dense woods. Redwood is also unusual in that it is considered an effective nonconductor of electricity when dry.

Architects find redwood is very flexible in many applications inside and outside. Finer grade redwood is probably used more in exteriors than in interiors, with commercial and institutional construction using more than residential construction. Redwood is also used in the manufacture of lawn furniture, flower and planter boxes, spa and hot tub surrounds, birdhouses, wine racks, and many other products.

Rustic sidings

Knotty redwood sidings are less expensive than the finer architectural grades. They are available in most standard redwood patterns, including extra-thick, $1^1/4$-inch bevel and rabbeted bevel. The thicker patterns are more stable and hold knots better. Rustic siding is intended only for exterior use.

Some building authorities suggest that redwood siding not be used with rigid plastic foam sheathing. In many cases, the rigid foam sheathing is not recommended for use with air-seasoned and unseasoned sidings.

Board and batten redwood

Many board and batten wall patterns can be created using stock-milled redwood lumber. These include various battens: overwide boards, equally spaced board and batten, and reverse board and batten, which resembles a channel pattern. It should only be installed vertically with a minimum 1-inch board lap. Any redwood grade can be used with this type of siding.

Redwood sidings are available in all the standard designs as well as the more artistic or architectural patterns. Shiplap, bevel, tongue and groove, and finger-jointed shapes are among them.

CEDAR

There are many differences in cedar shakes and shingles including a great variance in pricing. In most cases, the thickness and the grade of the siding determine the price.

PLYWOOD LAP

One fairly recent product available for use in siding is plywood lap siding. It comes in a variety of lengths and widths, but among the most popular panels are the 16-foot lengths and the 8-inch widths.

Plywood lap siding is installed over traditional wall framing covered with building paper or sheathing. For best results, wall studs should be spaced no more than 16 inches on center.

If you do not use rigid sheathing, you must install let-in bracing, which consists of 2×4s angle cut and running from the sole plate to the top plate of the wall framing. The sole plate is the timber that forms the bottom of the wall frame, and the top plate is the timber, usually a 2×4 in both cases, that covers the studs at the top of the wall frame.

Let-in bracing is installed starting at the corner post of the wall. From the corner post, measure out 8 feet along the sole plate and mark the location. Strike a chalk line from the top of the corner post to the point where you made the mark 8 feet from the post. The mark will cross several studs.

Next, angle-cut several lengths of 2×4s and nail these from the corner post to the first stud—aligned with the chalk line—and the second from the first stud to the second. Continue this way along the length of the chalk line until you have crossed five studs. The final length will be fitted at the corner or angle formed by the sixth stud and the sole plate. Do this on both sides of the corner. See FIG. 3-1.

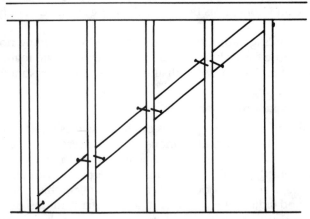

3-1 When installing let-in bracing for corners, follow a chalk line on both corner walls. Cut several lengths of bracing to use between studding and nail as shown.

An alternative to using let-in bracing is to install a panel of plywood (full 4-×-8-foot panels) as corner bracing. If you use plywood corners, you do not need any other form of bracing. See FIG. 3-2.

3-2 If you don't want to use plywood at corners, use metal bracing and then install rigid foam insulation on top.

When the corners are secured adequately, you are ready to start installing the siding, provided you have already installed the building paper or foam sheathing. Start by nailing in place a starter strip. This starter strip, or watershed, is a 1 × 2 that runs along the wall line where the framing meets the foundation wall. The strip causes the siding to slope outward so that rain and other moisture is shed quickly as it runs down the wall. See FIG. 3-3.

Measure from the top of the wall frame to the wall line at each corner of the wall to be certain that the distance is the same. If the measurements are satisfactory, you can use a line level and chalk line to get the proper location for the starter strip.

Corner boards should be installed before you start applying siding. To apply corner boards, position 1 × 4s (or wider, if your needs are such) over the corners so that you can install the plywood lap siding between the boards at each corner of the wall. Measure the distance between the corner posts and cut siding, if necessary, to fit between the boards.

If you are using 16-foot plywood lap siding, you will probably need to install one full length and then cut the next piece to fit. Nail the ends of the first section of siding to the corner post on one end and halfway across a stud at the other end. For best results, always end a section of siding over a stud. Do not let the end cross more than halfway across the stud if you are to butt another section of siding against the one just installed.

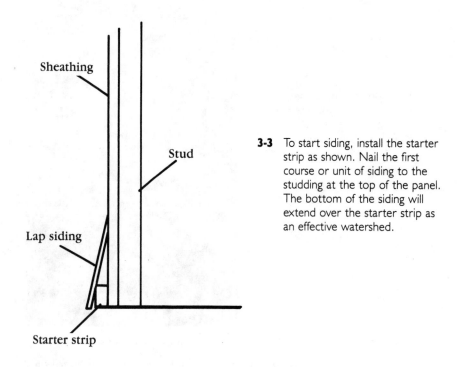

Sheathing

Stud

Lap siding

Starter strip

3-3   To start siding, install the starter strip as shown. Nail the first course or unit of siding to the studding at the top of the panel. The bottom of the siding will extend over the starter strip as an effective watershed.

Let the first course of plywood lap siding extend below the wall line by 2 inches. The purpose of this lap is to keep moisture from entering the wall between the framing and the foundation wall.

Nail through the plywood and into every stud on the wall. Do not nail the bottom of the plywood. When the first course is completed, add the second course. Decide the amount of lap you want, but do not allow less than 2 inches of lap. Measure down 2 inches from the top of the first unit of siding and mark the spot. Do the same thing at the other end. Then strike a chalk line between the two marks. See FIG. 3-4.

When you install the second course, let the bottom of the unit align exactly with the chalk line then nail the unit in place as you did before. Repeat the chalk line process for the third unit, or course. Do this all the way to the top of the wall.

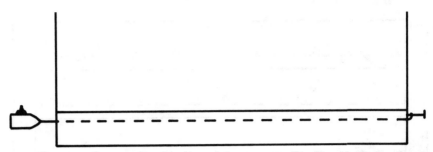

3-4 Mark the chalk line slightly below the wall line. Install the starter strip so that the bottom of the strip is aligned with the chalk line.

When two units join in one course, do not lap the ends. Butt one end against the other. Measure from the top of the top plate to the top of the most recently installed course. Do this regularly to be sure that you are maintaining the proper spacing.

If you are leaving 6 inches to the weather, with 2 inches lapped for watershed, measure the remaining distance in inches and then divide by 6 to see how many more courses are needed. When you are halfway or more up the wall and you have 4 feet left, convert this into 48 inches and divide by 6. At this time, you know there is room for eight more courses to have a perfect fit.

If you have 50 inches, you realize that you need to either lap more or less in order to have a good fit at the top. You must absorb 6 inches in extra lap or expand 4 more inches in order to have a perfect fit at the top.

If you choose to absorb the extra 2 inches, start lapping by $1/4$ inch less. After eight courses, you'll have absorbed the 2 inches. This $1/4$-inch difference in the lap will not be readily noticeable and you will still have good moisture resistance.

If you need to make room for another full course, you have 4 inches to eliminate. You can start lapping slightly more on each course. By lapping $2^1/2$ inches rather than 2 inches, you'll use the extra 4 inches and not have to install a thin strip at the top or rip a unit to secure a good fit.

You might be able to plan your lap so that you will have a full-width course under windows. If you can't, hold the siding in place and mark where the window frame occurs. Measure to see how much of the siding needs to be cut out. Use a square to mark the cut, then cut out the marked section. If you are working alone, you can drive several nails partly into the plywood along the chalked line and then rest the next unit atop the nails. The nails will hold the siding while you mark it. You can also use nails for every course you install to keep the siding from sagging. See FIG. 3-5.

Always watch to see that the siding course does not fall below the chalked line. The key to a neat wall and exceptional appearance is to keep all courses level and even.

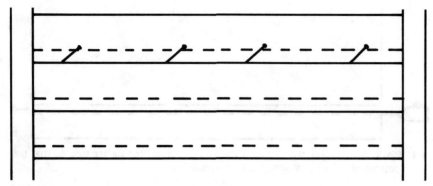

3-5 Drive two or three nails partly into the panel to hold the next unit of siding in position while you nail it.

Chapter 4

Shakes and rough siding

Two types of siding that can be used to create an interesting and attractive exterior wall covering are shakes, often referred to as cedar shakes or redwood shakes, and rough siding. The shakes or shingles are made of several different types of wood, but cedar remains one of the most popular, if expensive, woods used.

Rough siding can refer to a number of types of wood or simulated wood siding. Often, this siding is called rough sawn or rough hewn to indicate that one edge is irregular, just as if it had been cut from a log and not milled. Some sidings in this general classification are called barnboard or planked siding. Wood shakes also are classified as hand-split and resawn shakes, taper split shakes, and straight-split shakes.

Although you might find other lengths, shakes usually come in lengths of 16, 18, and 24 inches. They also come in widths of 3 inches up to 9 or 10 inches. One advantage of wood shingles is that they can be applied by anyone handy with basic tools, and there is little lifting to be done and no highly sophisticated tools are needed.

You can buy shingles or shakes with factory-grooved surfaces for ease in installation and factory-stained or painted shakes are also available. The range of possible products is wide enough that nearly every taste can be met.

Depending upon the supplier, you can even find wood shingles or shakes that are up to 14 inches in width. The shakes are often sold in random widths as well as in uniform widths.

Hand-split and resawn shakes derive their label from the fact that the faces are hand-split or have the hand-split look, while the backs are sawn. The shakes are produced by running boards through a bandsaw to split them and taper them to the desired thickness.

Taper split shakes are made by a craftsman using a froe. A froe is a cutting instrument that consists of a long, thick blade that is sharp on the bottom and flat on the top. At the end of the froe blade there is a circle for a handle, which extends upward at a right angle when the froe is held correctly. A maul or wooden hammer is used to drive the blade through the wood from which the shingles are to be split.

Even today, shingles are handmade. Start with a round length of straight-grained wood, such as oak or cedar. The wood should be tough, hard, and durable. Softer woods like poplar and pine do not last well if unprotected from the weather.

With the round length of log in front of you, use an axe or maul and wedge to split off the shingle sides of the length of wood. You will be left with a square-sided rectangular length of wood.

Stand the rectangle or cube on edge and place the blade of the froe so that it is parallel to the edge of the wood and at the desired thickness. Firmly hammer the top edge of the froe until the blade begins to sink into the wood and the wood starts to split.

As soon as the splitting begins, pull the handle backward, causing the shingle to split the rest of the way until it is free of the wood. See FIG. 4-1. After you have cut two or three shingles, lift the base wood and turn it over and split from the other end to retain the tapered effect needed.

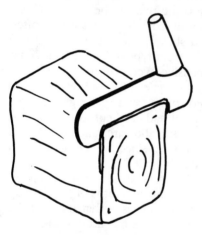

4-1 This illustration shows how a froe is positioned on a block of wood. Hit the back of the blade, and when the shingle starts to split away, pull on the handle to spring the shingle free.

Under normal circumstances, the first shingle will be slightly thicker on one end than on the other. If you do not up-end the base wood, the thickness of the shingles will be uniform and you will not have the tapered look in the installation process. When you use tapered shingles, the shingles tend to fit rather flatly against the wall.

If you make your own shingles, you will find that it might take you several minutes for each shingle. If your wood is straight-grained, and if you learn to use the froe effectively, you will soon be able to split a shingle in seconds. It is commonly said that an expert craftsman can make up to 1,000 shingles in one day's work.

As a beginner, you might feel fortunate to make 50 or so shingles in a day. As you continue to work, your speed will increase as your knowledge of wood grains and the leverage of the froe increases.

Straight-split shingles are also made with a froe. The major difference is that there is no tapering. You keep the thickness uniform by not up-ending the base section of wood. These shingles tend to fit against the wall less snugly than tapered shingles, but the look is not undesirable. There is a place for all three basic types of shingles, depending on the tastes of the builder.

INSTALLING SHAKES

When you install shingles, you can, for easy installation, butt-nail the shakes. This means nailing the shakes at the top end, or butt, rather than at the bottom end. By butt-nailing, you keep nails from showing and from being exposed to the weather.

To begin, you can use either double-coursing or sheathing boards as a backing for the shingles. In double-coursing, you nail up two layers of shingles. A poorer grade of shingle is nailed onto the wall first and the better grade is then nailed on top of the first layer. You must have plywood sheathing under the shingles or you will not have a good backing for the wall. Rigid foam sheathing will break if you try to nail shingles to it.

If you want to use sheathing boards, you can install boards spaced properly so that each course of shingles will end with the butts resting on the boards. Use felt construction paper between the sheathing and the studding or between the shingles and the sheathing.

The type of installation you choose will depend largely on the climate. In colder climates, do not use sheathing boards. If you use sheathing boards, install the first one along the wall line and the second one the length of the shingles above the first one. If you are using 16-inch shingles, then nail the sheathing boards 15 inches above the first one. See FIG. 4-2.

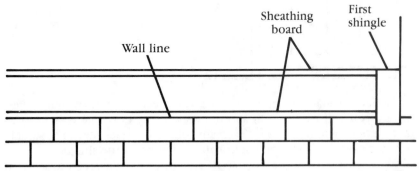

4-2 Note the position of the sheathing boards. The shingle should end slightly below the bottom sheathing board so that the wall line is covered.

You will need to double-course the first row. Nail in the first shingle so that the edge is flush with the corner post of the wall and so that the bottom end laps over the wall line by an inch or so. Nail the shingle at the top and the bottom, with two nails at each end. Nail the second shingle so that the edge is positioned against the first one. Nail it the same way. See FIG. 4-3.

When the first course is completed, you'll notice that there are slight spaces between shingles that could easily admit moisture and wind. At this point, install the second or double course of shingles so that the shingles lap over the cracks between the first ones.

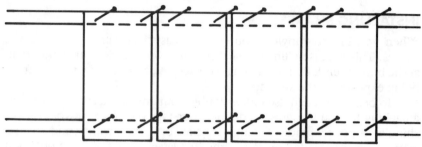

4-3 When you are double coursing, nail shingles with two nails at the top and two at the bottom. Leave a small space for expansion between the shingles.

You can use a wide shingle that will reach from the corner post outer edge to the middle of the second shingle or you can start with a narrow shingle that will reach only halfway across the first shingle. The second shingle will then reach to the midpoint of the next shingle. This way, you complete the first course all the way to the opposite corner post. See FIG. 4-4.

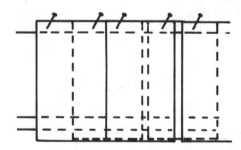

4-4 After the first course is nailed in place, start the second course so that each gap of the first course is lapped, or covered by, the shingles of the second course.

When you start the second course, you must decide how much overlapping you will need. From another viewpoint, how many inches "to the weather" will there be on each shingle. Remember that each shingle will be lapped from the top about half the length of the shingle.

This might seem like a waste of shingles, but you need to keep in mind that if you don't lap at least halfway, there will be a crack that will permit moisture and wind to enter the wall. If your shingles are 16 inches long, the next sheathing board should be no more than 7 or 8 inches from the board below it. See FIG. 4-5.

When you start to install the second course, let the shingle overlap half the length of the first course. Butt nail the shingle by nailing each top

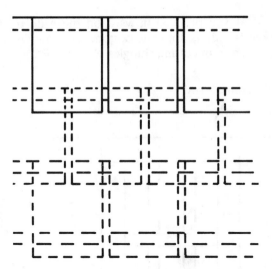

4-5 As you move up the wall, each shingle should completely cover the gap between shingles in the row below. This means that at least half of each shingle is used for lapping.

corner to the sheathing board. Position the second shingle against the first, and continue in this way across the wall.

Notice that there is a crack between the upper halves of the shingles. When you are ready for the third course, the shingles will lap over the cracks and close them. This same pattern will continue to the top of the wall.

When you double-course a wall, use lower grade shingles for the first course and let the ends extend slightly below the wall line. When you nail the second course over the first thickness, let the end of the top shingles extend an inch or so below the end of the first shingles.

Follow this same pattern up the wall so that cracks are lapped and so that the ends of the top or surface shingles—the ones that will show when the work is done—always extend below the ends of the lower-grade course. The purpose of this technique is to keep the lower-grade shingles from showing. You can stagger the ends of the shingles for a more rustic look. To do this, let every other shingle extend about 4 inches below its neighbor. There are other basic patterns that can be used. See FIG. 4-6.

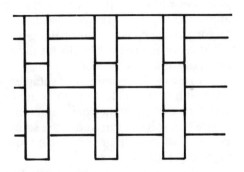

4-6 You can create your own rustic arrangement for shingle installation. The staggered effect is attractive and very popular.

As you proceed upward on the wall, try to line up the sheathing boards with the tops and bottoms of windows. The purpose of this plan is to keep from cutting shingles. See FIG. 4-7.

Sheathing board

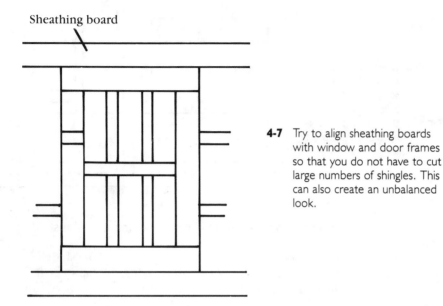

4-7 Try to align sheathing boards with window and door frames so that you do not have to cut large numbers of shingles. This can also create an unbalanced look.

SHINGLE AND SHAKE PANELS

You can buy shingle and shake panels if you prefer this method of installing shingles on walls. These panels consist of a backing material to which shingles have been glued or bonded permanently. You can find these panels in 8-foot lengths and in factory-stained finishes. Unstained panels are also available.

The courses in each panel are usually 7 inches, which gives a 14-inch height as well as the 8-foot length. The cost of these panels is somewhat higher than enough shingles to cover the same space, but the economy of the panel purchase is realized in the time saved during installation.

If you are paying workers to help with the installation, the money you save will offset the extra cost of the shingles. These panels can be applied in the same way you would install other shingles. The major difference in nailing is that butt-nailing is not done, and you will need to buy color-matched nails to blend with the color of the panels, which are most often of western red cedar.

To estimate the amount of shingles needed, multiply the length times the width of the wall. Do not deduct for windows and doors. The waste will probably equal the space difference provided by the windows.

When you have arrived at the square footage of the wall or walls to be covered, ask your dealer how many squares or how many shingles will be needed for the job.

You can learn how many square feet will be covered by one square of shingles. A square consists of four bundles of shingles, and the number of shingles needed will be determined by the amount of shingle to the weather. Keep in mind that usually half of a shingle will be overlapped.

If you are using 16-inch shingles that are 8 inches wide, you can cover about 180 square feet with four bundles. If the shingles are 18 inches long and 6 inches wide, you can cover about 109 square feet. If the shingles are 24 inches long and 10 inches wide, you can cover 133 square feet.

ROUGH AND BATTEN SIDING

There are several types of rough or batten siding. While the terms themselves suggest one style of siding, you can easily include plywood, hardboard, and rough-cut or milled boards.

If you install vertical siding composed of boards, these boards are usually no more than 8 inches wide. These rough boards are installed with battens used to cover the cracks between the boards. Such siding is called board-and-batten siding.

You can also use batten installed over plywood and similar materials to provide a board and batten look. This type of installation provides a rustic look that has enjoyed such popularity in recent years.

It is possible to combine any two or more of the basic siding materials to produce a wide variety of siding effects. You can mix brick and wood, brick and vinyl, wood and vinyl, and a number of similar materials for a look that is original and unique as well as effective and attractive.

When you install board and batten siding, you will need to start by adding backing blocks between the studding of the wall frame. Without backing blocks, there would be a nearly 16-inch wide space with no support anywhere from the top cap of the wall to the sole plate. This, in turn, means that the boards can be nailed only at the top and at the bottom, with no support in between. You would have nearly 8 feet of unsupported siding.

The solution is to install two backing blocks between studs at every point along the wall. These are best located one-third and two-thirds of the distance from sole plate to top cap. See FIG. 4-8. Divide the distance between the top and bottom of the studs by three. Assume you have studs that are fully 8 feet from top to bottom or, more accurately, from the top

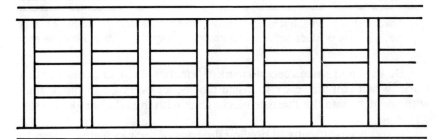

4-8 When you install backing blocks, divide the wall into thirds and install the top blocks 1/3 the way down the studding and the second blocks 2/3 the way down.

of the top cap to the bottom of the sole plate. You have 96 inches of space. Divide this number by 3 and you get 32 inches.

The first backing block should come 32 inches down the stud from the top of the top cap. The second backer block should come 64 inches from the top of the top cap. It is easier to install the blocks if you stagger them the thickness of a 2×4. This way, you can nail through the studs and into the end of the blocks. If you don't stagger them, you'll need to angle-nail or toe-nail every block into place, and this type of nailing is difficult for many beginners.

Block material should come from 2-×-4 stock. If possible, use short lengths that have been left over from other work to cut waste. Start at the corner post and measure the distance between the inside of the corner post and the near edge of the stud. Cut the 2-×-4 stock for the best fit possible.

If you cut the blocks too short or too long, you will cause the studs to bend or bow as you install the blocks. Use a level occasionally to determine that studs remain true and vertical.

An easy way to mark for installation of blocks is to strike a chalk line from one wall to the next. Let the chalk line cross the inside or outside edges of the studding. Measure down 32 inches from the top of the top cap on each end of the wall and mark the locations or drive a small nail partially in and then loop the chalk line over the nail and pull the line to the other mark. Hold the line taut and snap it.

Then align each block with the line. You can align so that the top of the block is aligned with the mark or so that the center of the bottom of the block is aligned. What matters is that you use the same alignment process each time. See FIG. 4-9.

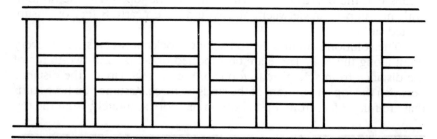

4-9 If backing blocks are staggered, you can nail them to the studs easier. Note that all blocks at interior studs can be nailed straight through the studs and into the ends without toenailing.

Go back and strike a second mark 1¹/₂ inches above or below the first mark. When you are ready to install blocks, let every other block align with one mark and the alternate blocks align with the other mark. See FIG. 4-10.

If you have difficulty in holding the ends of the block steady, stand a length of 2×4 or other lumber against the stud or the corner post and let the end of the block rest on the piece of lumber. You can use the same

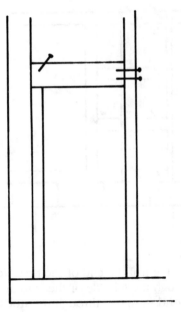

4-10 A support timber allows the backing block to rest on it while you nail. Toenail into the corner post and end-nail through the studding.

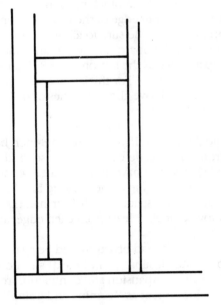

4-11 A small block under the backing block support allows you to use the same support for all block nailing.

length of support lumber against all the studs for that particular alignment. See FIG. 4-11.

For the alternate blocks, stand the length of lumber on top of a scrap block of 2×4 and then lay the blocking on top as you did before. The scrap 2×4 will bring the alignment to the correct level. See FIG. 4-12.

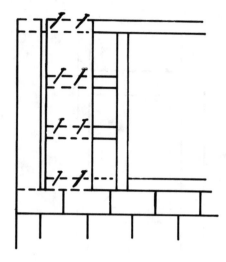

4-12 Boards installed vertically have four nailing points. Use them all for a sturdy installation.

Toe-nail the end of the first block into the corner post and then nail through the far side of the stud and into the end of the blocking. At the second stud, nail through the studs and into the end of the block at both locations. Continue to do this until you reach the other end of the wall, where you will need to nail one end into the corner post.

When all the blocking is in place, start installing the vertical boards. Let the bottom edge of the boards extend slightly past the wall line, about an inch or so. Be sure to allow the same spacing for all boards.

Nail the boards at the top and bottom by driving in two nails at the top and two at the bottom. Use 8-d nails for thinner boards such as 1 inch or five-quarters. For thicker boards, use longer and thicker-shanked nails. You should have about 2 inches of nail inside the studding to assure a firm hold.

Drive two nails through the board and into each of the backing blocks as well. If you are using 8-inch boards, drive the first nail 2 inches from the outside edge and the second nail also 2 inches from the other edge. You will have approximately 4 inches of space between the nails.

Do the same at the backing blocks. If the boards are wider, use three nails evenly spaced at all four nailing points. If the boards are narrow, allow an inch at least from each edge and then space the nails evenly. See FIG. 4-13.

The second board should be spaced about half an inch from the first one, and all subsequent boards should be similarly spaced. The purpose is to allow expansion and contraction room. Old-time builders referred to this movement as "coming and going" of the boards. See FIG. 4-14.

When all boards are installed, go back and nail in the batten strips over the cracks. These strips are usually about 2 inches wide and 1 inch thick. Space nails so that you can hit the boards behind the batten strips and yet leave enough room on the edge of the batten so that there will be no splitting.

Note that you do not omit sheathing under the board and batten sid-

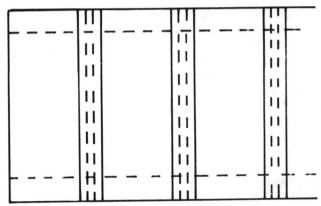

4-13 Nail batten strips every foot or so over the gaps between vertical siding boards. Nails should be large enough to hold well but not large enough to split the wood.

4-14 This siding came from the decking of a century-old mill. Lumber was free to anyone who could carry it away.

ing. You will need to use all the basic insulation and sheathing that you would normally use.

If you want to use plywood or another composition material, install it as you normally would and then nail the batten over the joints. If you want a board-and-batten look, divide the width of the plywood or composition material by three and nail batten at the proper locations.

This means that your batten will be nailed over studs. If the composition material is 48 inches long, the first batten will occur at the joint. The second will be 16 inches from the joint, and the third will occur 32 inches from the joint. The fourth will occur at the edge of the plywood where the next joint will occur.

The batten addition will lend a.. appearance of siding boards that are 16 inches wide. Much exterior plywood is grooved at intervals to provide the board look. You can omit the batten at these points if you wish, but often the result is far more attractive if you use the same type of batten across the entire wall.

One very inexpensive and incredibly superior board-and-batten installation process can be achieved if you can locate some old building that is being demolished and make a deal for the decking from the building. Such decking is often 3½ inches thick and up to 12 inches wide. This excellent thickness provides amazing insulation as well as strength, durability, and a strong measure of sound-proofing.

Old mills, schoolhouses, and public buildings provide the very best decking, and often the owners of such buildings will give the materials to anyone who is willing to remove them and haul them away. You can also make a deal with the owner that you will demolish the building in exchange for the materials. He will then save money and you will receive free building materials.

If you happen upon such a bonanza, you can install the board siding as suggested, and then for batten, use full-width decking lapped over the joints. Such a wall will be 7 inches thick and will contain such insulation power that your savings in heating and cooling will be worth all the trouble required to salvage and install the decking. See FIGS. 4-15 through 4-18.

4-15 Note the diagonal installation under windows and the use of curved windows for a unique effect.

4-16 For variety and uniqueness, angles of diagonal installation for the deck railing and a vertical installation for the siding was used. Full-width batten boards were used to lap the first board joints.

4-17 Short lengths of siding boards were installed diagonally to lend a distinctive air to this utility building.

4-18 Leftover decking boards from the outside siding are bolted together to create girders for open ceilings. The boards tie the decor of the outside of the house with the inside.

One note about salvaged material: most building codes will not permit you to use salvaged lumber for load-bearing purposes. You can use it for siding, however, without question, and it can be used for interior wall coverings, doors, railings, and other needs in your building projects—except for load-bearing walls.

If you have siding boards left over, these can often be bolted together and used for girders in exposed-beam construction. You can also use such timbers for garages, workshops, and other out-buildings.

If you must buy your own siding boards, consider rough-sawn boards. These boards are very economical and provide a beautiful rustic look.

Chapter **5**

Stone siding

One of the oldest and most attractive building materials in man's history is stone or rock. While it is not at the top of the list of most popular building materials, stone can be among the most beautiful of materials, and there is an immense versatility and majesty connected with rock that is missing in nearly all other building materials. See FIG. 5-1.

There are several reasons for the lack of immense popularity of stone as a building material. First, stone can be expensive to buy and to install. Second, stone might be hard to obtain in some areas of the country and transportation can be expensive. Third, stone has the reputation of being hard to work with.

Several basic elements of these arguments are valid. Even when stone is readily available, the quality might not be as great as it should be. Many brick or concrete block masons dislike working with stone.

Their reasons are also valid. Many block masons and brick masons are paid by the number of units they lay. Many years ago, block masons were paid $1 per block laid, and a good mason could lay well over 100 blocks in a day. Similarly, a brick mason who is experienced and energetic can earn a great deal of money in one day's time.

A rock mason does not enjoy the uniformity of shape that can be found in bricks and blocks. While all bricks in a certain style are virtually the exact same size, rocks are rarely the same size and shape.

A rock mason will, of necessity, spend a great deal of time selecting the best rock for the spot to be filled. He will also devote a large part of his working day to cutting or chipping or shaping rocks to fit the spaces that must be filled.

These arguments can also be seen from a radically different viewpoint. Because stone masons are somewhat hard to find or difficult to hire, stone or rock houses are also somewhat rare, and the person who

5-1 Stone masonry can create some of the most original and unique houses in contemporary building.

builds a beautiful stone house will find that he has a showplace home that is admired and envied by thousands of people.

The home builder who wants his house to be unique can find the singular appearance he desires in stone very frequently. While all brick houses of the same design tend to look very similar, nearly all stone houses have a distinctive look.

When you decide to face your house with stones, you also have to make a basic choice of using natural field stone or quarried and cut stone. If you choose to use commercially produced stone, you can do the work yourself with little difficulty. If you want to use field stone, you will need to approach the job in a different manner and from a different starting point. With commercially produced stone, you can start at the top and work your way down. With natural stone, you need to start at the bottom and work upward.

Field stones are laid in the true sense of masonry. Commercial stone work is actually stuck onto the existing wall. Natural stones rest on the stones below them and on a bed of mortar. Commercial stones do not rest on anything at all. They are held in place by the cement and mortar mixture and then the spaces between stones are filled in with mortar after the rocks are in place. See FIG. 5-2.

If this description is confusing, think in terms of short lengths of thick wood, such as foot-long lengths of 2×10s. You can stack the wood, one piece on top of another and create a low wall. You can also nail the pieces to an existing wall and soon cover the entire wall.

5-2 Many houses combine contemporary styling with rock or stone masonry.

The same is essentially true of stone, with the so-called rubble stone being laid like oblong bricks or blocks while the processed stones are stuck like the nailed wood could be. Both walls are serviceable and effective as well as attractive.

Rubblestone walls are much stronger than stuck-on stone walls, which are only as strong as the wall behind the stone facing. You will most likely use a concrete block wall behind the stones, so your wall will be very strong and durable. See FIG. 5-3.

In 1989, a fierce tornado swept through a small North Carolina town and totally demolished brick churches and houses as well as frame houses and outbuildings. One of the few structures left standing was a rubblestone chicken house. The roof was torn off of the house but not a single stone was dislodged. The walls remained as firm and strong as they did before the tornado, although the major force of the twister scored a direct hit on the chicken house and destroyed all the other buildings on the farm.

5-3 Combining styles makes for interesting architecture. Here, a random or rubble-stone wall is used with wood siding.

BUYING STONE

You can find many suitable stones in fields, along streams or stream beds, and in woodland areas. Searching for these stones and then carrying them to your truck and then transporting them to the building site is time-consuming and energy-consuming. You might find it much easier simply to call your masonry supply dealer and order the stone or rock you need.

You might be asked how many stones or rocks you will need for the job, but most of the time you can tell the dealer the size of the job you are planning and he can estimate the amount of stone you will need. If you are dealing with an inexperienced salesperson, you can calculate the necessary stones easily.

For a rubble or courses wall, multiply the height of the wall in feet times the length of the wall in feet times the thickness of the wall in feet. Then divide the number you reach, the quotient, by 27.5 for the number of perches of stone you will need. For example, a wall 20 feet long, 12 feet high, and 6 inches thick would be:

$$20 \times 12.5 = 120$$
$$120 \div 27.5 = 4 \text{ to } 5 \text{ perches}$$

A perch of stone is a measure of about 25 cubic feet of stone. More accurately, you will receive 24^1/$_2$ cubic feet of stone, but the mortar and filling will account for another 2^1/$_2$ cubic feet of wall coverage to give a total of about 27 or 27^1/$_2$ feet of coverage. When you divide the number of cubic feet needed by 27.5 you are dividing the total footage by the amount of space one perch will cover.

You can also buy stone by the cord. A cord is 128 cubic feet of stone, but you will also have mortar and filling, which will bring the total to 156 cubic feet. To find the number of cords needed for a wall, multiply the length, height, and thickness of the wall in feet and divide by 156. The answer will provide you with the number of cords needed.

If you need to consider the load-bearing capacity of a footing, keep in mind that one cubic foot of stone will weigh between 130 and 175 pounds. If a wall is 20 feet long, 12 feet high, and 1 foot thick, you will have 540 cubic feet. At the very least, the wall will weigh about 60,000, and at the very most, it will weigh nearly 70,000 pounds. If you divide the number by 12, you will find that your wall will weigh about 5,800 pounds per linear foot.

If the wall is thinner than 1 foot, it will weigh less. A 6-inch wall will weigh 2,900 pounds per foot, and a 3-inch wall will weigh approximately 950 pounds per linear foot.

Stone is available in several grades and it is a good idea for you to get samples of each grade. If you ungraded stone, you might find that some of the individual stones are 6 inches thick, while others are only 1 inch thick. The result of such lack of uniformity will be a wall that is highly irregular on the face and unsightly by most standards.

If you buy a good grade of stones, you can split some of the rocks and nearly double your coverage or, seen another way, cut the cost of the rock facing by half at best. More importantly, you'll get a better-looking wall. See FIG. 5-4.

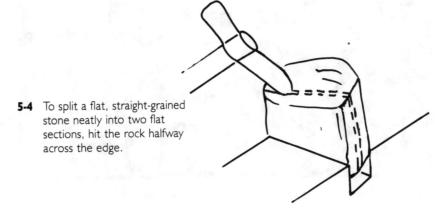

5-4 To split a flat, straight-grained stone neatly into two flat sections, hit the rock halfway across the edge.

LAYING RUBBLE STONE WALLS

The two types of stone walls most frequently built from natural stone are rubble and ashlar walls. Ashlar stones are squared and cut to resemble rather uniform blocks of essentially the same size and shape, although certain variations are allowed for uniqueness in appearance. Rubble stone walls are left in their natural shape; no cutting or squaring in any form is done.

Either type of wall can be course-layed or random-layed. See FIGS. 5-5 and 5-6. Course laying means that the stones are laid in rows that are more

5-5 Course-laid stones are laid so that there is some bonding created. The rocks do not rest on each other but the mortar joints bind the courses together.

5-6 Random-laid stones are laid without pattern, course line, or bonding.

or less even and continuous. Random laying means that no effort at courses or patterns is made.

To start a rubble stone wall, you must begin with a footing of some sort. This footing is often an open trench that is filled with long and narrow rocks laid end to end until the bottom of the trench is covered. The rocks can be as thick as you like or as thick as you can manage.

You can also dig a footing trench and pour concrete footings. Check with the building inspector before you use the stone footing, and be sure to have the inspector check the footing trench even if you plan to use concrete.

One building inspector checked a southern house that was to be built on a rock covered with a few feet of dirt. The excavator could not move or even damage the rock, and the building inspector accepted the rock as the footing. His comment was that, if a back hoe could not budge the rock, the weight of the house was not going to create problems.

Both concrete and rocks will crack. Sometimes, the cracking is caused by excessive pressure on the rocks, and at other times, the cause is poor weather conditions when the concrete was poured.

Concrete has the advantage of continuing to harden even for years after it is poured. The chairman of the civil engineering department at a college near Charlotte, North Carolina pointed out that concrete might actually harden more each year for as long as a century before the hardening finally stops.

Rock is usually as hard as it will ever be when you use it as a footing, but you should remember that the rock has been in a tempering process for perhaps thousands of years. Seen in this light, it is reasonable to assume that either material will give long and efficient service.

When the footing is prepared, you are ready to start laying rubble stone. You will need to use the biggest stones at the bottom, for several reasons. One reason is that the larger stones will give greater support to the smaller stones above it. A second reason is that the weight of the larger stones creates difficulties for the mason who must place them high in the wall.

Start by laying a mortar bed on top of the footing stones or concrete. Then use the widest and longest stones that will fit into the footing and wall. If you want a wall that is 12 inches thick, then choose stones that are a foot wide and as long as you can find or handle. A stone 4 feet long, as long as it is strong and sound, works well.

Always be sure that the footing stones are as long as the wall is wide. Lay all rocks so that the broadest face is turned down. Do not lay a rock that is precariously balanced before the mortar is applied. Each rock you use should lie reasonably flat and stably if you simply position the dry rock in place.

Lay the footing stones in the mortar bed and completely cover the footing surface with mortar at least 1 inch thick. Fill in any small holes that are open in the footing and then cover the footing stones with a mortar bed in order to lay the second course of stones.

Keep selecting large stones for the second and third courses. Lay these stones so that the outer edge of the wall is kept as even as possible. If a stone fits well except for a sharp projecting lip, you can use a hammer to knock off the projection.

Examine rocks for color uniformity or patterned contrast. You can lay aside rocks that you know will fit in a particular point later. Set aside rocks that are oddly colored unless you desire the sharp contrast.

BONDING

Bonding in stone work is as important as it is in brick or block work. A bond header should be used regularly in rubble stone work. To install a bond stone, locate a stone that is wide enough to reach across the entire wall's thickness. You can use stones that reach only halfway across for the rest of the course but the bond stone should cover the entire surface width of the wall.

This bond header that you are installing will cover all of the smaller stones in that part of the wall and will provide strength and produce an attractive pattern. If you decide to use bond headers every fourth course, try to use rocks that are essentially the same size and shape, although length is unimportant as long as the stone is as long as the width of the footings. See FIG. 5-7.

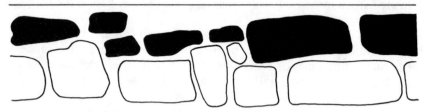

5-7 The shaded stones are bond headers. Note that each of the darker stones will bond with the two stones below it when the mortar is added.

If you have small holes that stones will not fill, you can leave the openings until the course above it is laid. Then you can break smaller stones and use the pieces to fit into the openings. You can use the point of the trowel to throw mortar back into the hole and then push the stones into place. You can also lay a small mortar bed and then mortar the sides of the stone before putting it into position.

As the wall climbs, you can use metal supports for the stones. These wall ties are thin strips of serrated metal that can be bent easily. When you are ready to use them, fasten one end to the wall behind the stone wall and then bend the tie so that it lies across the top of a stone. Lay a mortar bed and embed the tie in the mortar before laying the rocks on top of the tie.

When the mortar dries, the tie will be secured to the block wall behind the stone masonry and also to the rock wall. These supports keep the wall from tending to tip outward as the soil under the footings settles, if it does.

You can also use a form of stretcher bonding as you progress along the wall. If you have a short expanse of small rocks, you can locate long and wide rocks that will cover several of the smaller ones. If you have two fairly large stones laid end to end, you can use a longer rock to reach from halfway across the first rock to a similar point halfway across the second rock.

This way, you can support the wall in two directions by using wall ties and stretcher bonding. You can add more stability by tilting uneven rocks slightly toward the wall behind the stone facing. Do not exaggerate the tilt but allow the large rock to slope 10 degrees or so, if tilt is necessary. If you can lay the rock perfectly flat, do so.

Before you begin work, you need to determine whether the stone you are using is absorbent or nonabsorbent. If the stone tends to absorb moisture, you must wet the surface of the stone before you lay it. If you do not wet the stone, the rock will absorb the moisture from the mortar before the mortar can set up, and what is left will be a very weak mortar that is dried or nearly dry and ready to crumble.

Nonabsorbent stones will not absorb moisture and you do not need to dampen the stone surface. As a rule, most stones found in and along creek or river beds will absorb moisture.

The best stones to use for wall siding are granite, limestone, sandstone, and slate. Remember that the larger your stones are, the less mortar you will need, and vice versa. If you have a natural source of rocks, you can save a great deal of money by using the larger stones.

When you position a stone, try to set it in place as gently and accurately as you can. Try not to move the stone once it has been set in the mortar.

SETTING STONES

When you buy or otherwise obtain processed stones, you will find that the rocks are flat and grained in a very noticeable manner. The grain runs along the flat surface of the rock so that you can actually split the rock evenly and smoothly.

You will find that you can greatly increase the yield of the stones you buy if you can split them. If a flat stone is the size of a huge pot lid and 4 inches thick, you can easily split the stone and get two stones. Even a 3 inch thick stone can be split, so that you will be able to cover far more surface than you had originally estimated. Don't try to split stones that are already thin, you'll only get stones that are weak and brittle.

Before you mix mortar for sticking stones, consult with your dealer and ask him what type of cement is best for the stone in your area. Masonry mortar is unacceptable. Use a cement mixture and cut the amount of sand normally used. If you would use a bag of mortar mix with 26 shovels of sand, use a cement mix with 13 to 14 shovels of sand.

When you are ready to stick the stone onto the wall, start at the top and work downward. The reason for this is that, first, the stones do not rest on lower ones at all and second, you are certain to drop mortar while you work, and the spilled mortar will stick to the stonework already done and mar the appearance.

You will need to set up a scaffold so that you can reach the top of the wall where you can work comfortably. Locate your first stones and decide which side you want to show, then butter the other side. Spread the mortar thickly across the entire back surface of the rock.

Hold the rock or stone in one hand as though you were carrying a large tray. Hold your hand so that the palm faces upward and the stone rests flatly on your palm. When you are ready, push the stone into the wall with gentle but sudden force. You virtually slap the stone against the wall. As soon as contact is made, push against the stone and give it a one-quarter turn. This movement is to create a vacuum seal under the stone. Hold the stone in place for several seconds. It should remain in place when you turn it loose.

If you want a flat surface against the top of the wall, have the top surface positioned at roughly a nine o'clock position when the contact with the wall is made. Then push hard inward and turn the rock until the top surface is at 12 o'clock.

When you stick the next stone, take care not to hit the one you have just set. Leave an inch or so of space between the stones and do not fill the space with mortar until later. See FIG. 5-8.

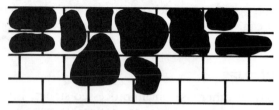

5-8 Do not mortar between stones until they have firmly adhered. Let the stones cure overnight before mortaring.

Work your way along the top of the wall, and when that part of the work is done, start sticking stones below the first ones. You should use stones at corners with a straight edge, just don't place the stone so that the edge is flush with the corner of the wall. Place the stone back an inch from the corner.

You might prefer not to place stones one under the other in a vertical line. Instead, you might prefer to center the lower stones between two upper stones. Vary the size and shape of the stones so that you do not have all the stones in a section the same size.

You can intentionally contrast the stones because when you try to keep uniform size and arrangement, you will not succeed unless the stones are precision-cut. So rather than have accidental variation, plan on intended variation.

Do not mix a great deal of mortar at one time. If the mortar dries out, discard it rather than try to moisten and re-mix it. If the mortar loses its adhesiveness, it will not hold the stones in place.

Work in one section to keep from moving the scaffolding across the length of the wall. Unlike pouring cement, you can stop sticking stones at any point.

After the stones have been stuck, allow them to dry for at least 24 hours before you mortar between the stones. If you want, you can stick all the stones on the building before you mortar between them. If any stones fall, scrape away the old mortar and spread new mortar on the back of the stone and re-stick it.

Occasionally, a stone will seemingly not stick to the wall. Try scraping off all the mortar that has been applied to the back of the stone and then re-butter the stone before sticking it again. If it still does not adhere to the wall, try dampening the stone. If nothing works, set the stone aside to use in a later project. Do not leave a stone that is clinging precariously, at best, to the wall.

Remember that people will frequently be near the wall after the work is completed and you do not want to take the chance that a stone will fall and injure someone or an article of personal property. If the troublesome stone adheres to the wall for a full day or even for two or three hours, it will probably remain in place without further incident.

APPLYING MORTAR

When all the stones are set and you have allowed them to "age" for a day or so, you are ready to apply mortar between the stones. This gives the wall a finished look. You might already know that you can buy cement in a modest variety of colors, and you can ask your dealer to provide additional information about the possible variety of shades.

Most dealers will not stock anything but the traditional gray or off-white cements. You can also find black cement in any store with a good stock of masonry materials. Ask the dealer to show you samples or at least photos of rock walls or traditional walls with rock facing filled with black mortar.

When you start to fill between the rocks, use cement rather than mortar mix. Black filler will often cost twice that of traditional cement, but you might decide that the final result in appearance is worth the extra money. See FIG. 5-9.

5-9 Dark mortar between rocks creates an effective visual impression that draws positive attention to the work.

Use a small trowel to apply the mortar. Use the side of the blade to cut into the mortar and lift one-fifth of a trowel load on the side of the trowel. Hold the trowel close to the space between stones and snap your wrist to sling the mortar into the space. It might be a good idea to practice on a low-visibility space before you work on more prominent parts of the wall.

Fill all around each and every stone. Fill the spaces deep enough so that you can spread the excess mortar slightly over the edges of the rocks. By covering the rock edges, you give the work the appearance of having perfectly fitted rocks at every point.

FINISHING TOUCHES

When rocks are started an inch or so from the corner of the cement or concrete block, there is a space that needs to be filled and rounded. This can be easily done by lifting a trowel load of mortar and slinging it gently into the vacant spaces. You can then use the trowel to smooth and shape the mortar. You do not actually round the mortar. Instead, you shape it or flatten it so that the finished corner has a rather slanted look rather than a sharp corner.

Use rocks of different sizes and shapes as you work. Don't try to fill every space with a rock but leave some mortar space. The mortar adds significantly to the finished appearance of the wall, and stones too close together appear excessively tight. Also, don't try to make the wall perfectly flat. The final effect is not nearly as attractive as slightly uneven surfaces.

Clean the rocks of all spilled mortar as you work. Don't let any mortar touch the surface of the rocks if you can help it. If clumps of mortar stick to stones, let it harden and then chip it off. You might need to use an

5-10   If you do not want to cover the whole wall with stones, cover portions of the house, such as window areas, as an attractive alternative.

acid cleanser to remove all the stains left by the mortar if the mortar is smeared badly across the face or surface of the stones.

You can apply rock siding to a house in several days of steady work, but if you are a beginner, you might be well advised to work slowly. Take your time, and wait to see if the patterns or color of mortar or the shapes of the rocks produced the effect you desired. You might decide that you don't want to cover the entire house with stones but would like stone accents. Perhaps you've chosen a bay window or other unique wall structure to lay stones around. See FIG. 5-10.

Chapter 6 covers material that is solid, versatile, and economical—concrete block.

Chapter 6

Concrete block walls

*L*aying concrete blocks can be one of the easiest projects associated with house construction. It can also be among the most difficult of jobs. Much depends on the physical condition of the worker and on the degree of involvement in the job.

It has been reported that more walls have been built from concrete blocks than from all other types of materials combined. This would include rock, brick, stone, marble, glazed tile, terra-cotta, and other similar materials. This observation might have been overstated if you consider the number of interior walls built in nearly every house. If the statement includes only exterior walls, it might be more readily accepted.

There are several reasons for the popularity of concrete block walls. They are durable, relatively inexpensive, and strong. They can also be built quickly (by experienced persons) and easily (if you follow basic guidelines carefully).

In terms of economy alone, concrete block walls are among the least expensive you can build. While cement blocks are not cheap, the exterior wall becomes the interior wall as well, and you save the money needed for interior wall construction. If you use a brick veneer exterior wall, you will need a wall frame for the interior walls. This frame is composed of 2-×-4 studding, wall plates, caps, and sole plates. The cost of the timbers, nails, and labor can add significantly to the cost of building, whether you are building a new home, adding a room, or even building a tool shed in the backyard.

Keep in mind that you also have the cost of the exterior brick veneer wall. Even if you cover the interior wall with paneling or drywall, you can apply or install the panels against the block wall and still save time, materials, and money. Finally, you can also apply a sealer and finish over a concrete block wall, allowing the wall to serve as both exterior and interior wall and thus save the money needed for interior wall covering. See FIG. 6-1.

6-1 Concrete block can be used for interior walls as well as exterior walls. Modern blocks are very attractive and create a very pleasant effect inside.

Another reason for the popularity of concrete block wall is that the art of laying blocks can be learned quickly and easily. The skills needed for laying walls for a residential dwelling can be mastered, at least to an acceptable degree, within a matter of hours. Don't assume that because you can build a wall for a house, you can handle the more advanced block-laying techniques. If you feel insecure about laying a masonry wall for your house, start by building a privacy wall for practice. Such a wall can be a very attractive part of your project (see FIG. 6-2).

6-2 Garden or privacy walls are good projects for gaining experience and confidence. Use as much care on fences as you would on the walls of your house.

Many houses have a foundation wall made of blocks that are later covered with pargeting or stucco, brick veneer, rocks, or some of the more modern materials on the market. See FIG. 6-3.

6-3 Even on houses of nontraditional design, concrete masonry figures are important. Piers, foundation walls, steps, and even stucco are all concrete masonry processes.

Another reason for the popularity of blocks in building is the wide variety of sizes and shapes of blocks. One manufacturer of concrete blocks reports that there are 2,000 different types of blocks, in terms of size, shape, and types. See FIG. 6-4.

You can buy blocks that vary in width from 4, 6, 8, 10, and 12 inches. The most common block heights are 4 inches and 8 inches. See FIG. 6-5.

Most blocks are 16 inches by 8 inches long. The actual length of blocks is slightly more than 15 inches, but with the mortar joint, the actual length becomes 16 inches.

ORDERING BLOCKS

Most American-made blocks have holes in them called cores, cavities, or air cells. Depending on the size of the block, most blocks will have either two or three cavities. See FIG. 6-6. You can buy blocks made from light-weight aggregate or common-weight aggregate. The actual weight of the various blocks will vary greatly, and if you are concerned about which to use, tell your dealer how you plan to use the blocks and he can recommend the type of blocks you will need for the job.

When you are ordering blocks, tell the dealer how many doors, windows, and other irregularities in the walls there will be. He might suggest that you buy reinforcing steel and lintel metal at the time you order.

When you order, tell the dealer first the width of the block, then the height, and finally the length. If you ask for a 12-×-8-×-16 block, you will be sent blocks that are 12 inches wide, 8 inches high, and 16 inches long. If you are confused on how to order, simply tell the dealer that you need

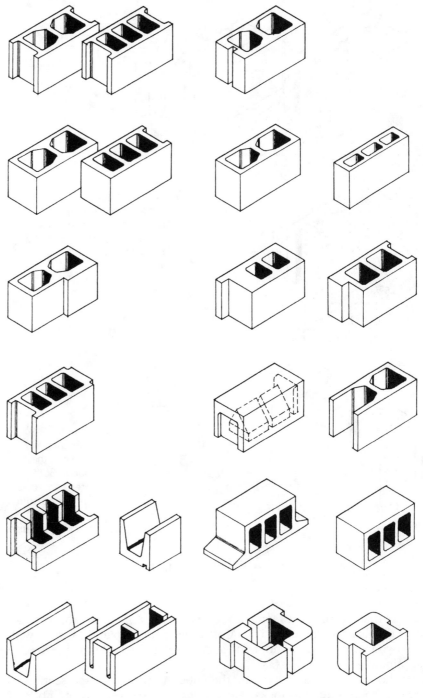

6-4 Some of the many types and designs of concrete block. There are blocks to suit nearly every building purpose.

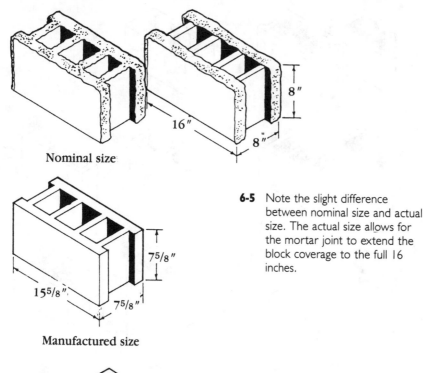

Nominal size

Manufactured size

6-5 Note the slight difference between nominal size and actual size. The actual size allows for the mortar joint to extend the block coverage to the full 16 inches.

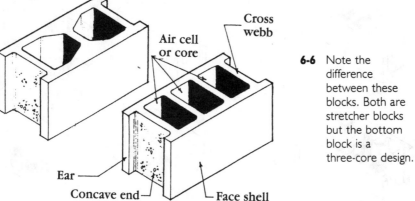

6-6 Note the difference between these blocks. Both are stretcher blocks but the bottom block is a three-core design.

blocks that are 16 inches long, 1 foot wide, and 8 inches high, or whatever the dimensions need to be. Most dealers are prepared to work with do-it-yourselfers and will not mind at all that you do not know the precise terminology.

Blocks are often ordered by the cube. A cube is a large section of blocks containing 90 blocks. Most firms will deliver any number of blocks beyond a minimal, so you do not need to buy an entire cube if you need only a fairly small number. If you need 115 blocks, the dealer will be happy to send you a cube and 25 loose blocks. Many dealers will also accept unused blocks if you need to return them. You might be asked to pay a small fee for the transportation of the blocks, however, or you can deliver them in a pickup truck if you own one or can borrow one.

When you order blocks, the delivery firm will set the blocks wherever you want them, as long as the terrain will permit, and you might need to be on hand when delivery is made. If you plan to lay a block foundation wall for a house, you might want to consider having the blocks set in the center of the work area. This way, you'll have blocks very near the work site, always within easy reach.

Have the blocks placed where they will not be muddied by work activities or weather. If you use dirty blocks, they will look unsightly, and if you return them, the dealer might be somewhat reluctant to accept soiled materials. Remember that you would not want to accept blocks that were muddy and dirt-covered, and the dealer might not want to ask his customers to accept them either.

MATERIALS AND EQUIPMENT

In addition to buying the blocks and insulation, you'll need a carpenter's level, framing square, chalk line, cord, and stakes. For mortar work, you'll need a trowel, mortar, a jointer, framing timbers, steel nails, and steel reinforcement wire (check your building codes). Steel wire comes in long sections (5 or 6 feet long) and 8 inches wide or slightly less. The logic behind the wire is to lock, or bond, the entire course together.

You will also need lintels for doorways and windows. You can buy lintels at hardware stores or concrete supply companies. To cut block, you'll need a hammer (a carpenter's hammer is optional), and a chisel set or a masonry blade for a circular saw.

When blocks, sand, and cement are delivered, protect them from the weather as much as you can. Remember that extremely wet sand can be difficult to mix into mortar, and in extremely cold weather, moist sand can freeze and become very hard to mix.

Cement also tends to absorb moisture, and if bags are left on the ground, the contents might set up or harden to the point that you cannot use them. Many dealers will not accept returns on concrete or mortar mixes. The dealers know that if the bags were left in the weather they may not be usable.

Any bags of cement that are not to be used immediately should be stored on platforms, boards, or pallets so they will not be in direct contact with the ground. The bags should also be covered with plastic or tarpaulin to keep rain off.

When your work rises beyond waist high, you might find that it is difficult to lift the 12-inch blocks, hold them aloft until they are positioned properly, and then gently set the blocks into position. You might need to construct some type of elevated work surface.

You can rent or build your own scaffolding. Either way, it is expensive, but it is usually necessary. When you set up the scaffold, attach all the connections so the scaffold will not shake and wobble while you work.

You will need boards to lay across the frame of the scaffold. These boards should be at least 2 inches thick and no less than 6 inches wide. A 10-inch board is safer. When three or four boards are laid side-by-side, you will have adequate support for the blocks you will need to lay there while you work.

You can also use three 2-×-6 timbers and then lay a sheet or panel of plywood across the boards. The plywood will give you a smooth footing and added strength for the job.

If you do not have access to scaffolding, you can construct a make-shift scaffold to use for low elevations. Do not try to work on such a scaffold at more that 5 or 6 feet high.

You can stack blocks at two points until you have a wall that is four feet wide and three or four feet high. Lay the boards across the formation and then add the plywood, if needed. You can work with reasonable safety in this fashion.

LAYING CORNERS

Blocks are laid in much the same way as bricks. You can think of a block as being a huge brick, with the major differences being size and weight. In many ways, blocks are easier to lay than bricks are, but you will learn quickly that the weight of large blocks can be a tiring task, particularly when you are laying higher courses. After footings are poured, you can start the corners of the wall. Many masons like to lay all four corners before they complete any of the courses. Use a chalk line, cord, and stakes to set off the starting points for each corner, and make certain that the four corners are all square.

You can check for squareness by running lines from stakes set on each side of the corner. The lines will run along two joining sides of the foundation wall lines. Check the point where the lines meet at the corner to see if the corner is square. Hold a framing square carefully with the blade and tongue each aligned with the two lines. The lines should be perfectly parallel with the two lines. If the lines are not parallel, you do not have a square corner. See FIG. 6-7.

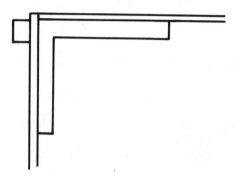

6-7 Use a square held lightly against the cords to see if the corners are square.

Another way to check for squareness is to measure from the corner out to a point along each line. If you measure out 6 feet along one line and 8 feet along the other line, the distance diagonally from point to point along the line should be 10 feet. See FIG. 6-8.

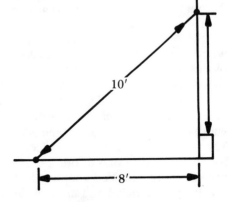

6-8 When you measure diagonally, do not push or pull the cord, you could get an incorrect reading.

Measure at all four corners to be sure that all corners are square. Another way of checking squareness is to measure from one corner diagonally across the house space to the other corner. Then measure the other way. Think of the house layout as having Corners A, B, C, and D. Measure diagonally from A to C and then from B to D. If the house layout is square, the two distances should be exactly the same. See FIG. 6-9.

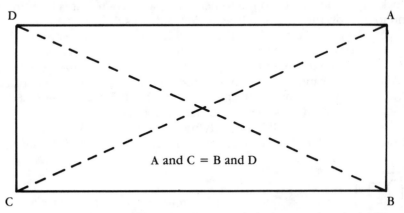

A and C = B and D

6-9 If the distance diagonally across the rectangle is the same from both directions, corners are square and footings can be poured.

Remember that, if your corners are off a fraction of an inch at the corner, the discrepancy will be several inches by the time you reach the other end of the wall line. Get the corners as nearly square as you can before you start to lay blocks.

When you are ready, measure the distance along two sides of the house, starting at one corner. Convert the distance into inches and divide by 16, the length of a block. If you planned your house well, the distance along the two sides of the house should be divisible by 16.

Assume that you are building a modest-sized house that is 40 feet long. Converted to inches, that distance is 480 inches. When you divide the number by 16, you learn that you will need 30 blocks to reach from corner to corner.

Do the same type of calculating for the other side of the house to see whether you can use whole blocks. You should also consider that the blocks will overlap by 8 inches at each corner. Of course, this calculating is done before your footings are poured.

If you have an odd length, you will have more waste of materials and time. Most drywall panels and other building materials come in 4-foot widths. Therefore, keeping dimensions divisible by 4 will simplify tasks. The side already figured is 40 feet, which means that you can use 30 blocks without having to break one, and you can also use 10 panels of drywall easily, provided your inside dimensions are 40 feet.

When the stakes and lines are in place, you will have a right angle where the first block will be laid. Use a chalk line to mark the external boundary for the blocks, and when you are ready, lay a bed of mortar along the chalk lines and then move inside by 12 inches (assuming that you are using 12-inch blocks) and lay another mortar bed.

Using the lines and the chalk marks as your guides, lay the first block so that it comes as close to the lines as possible without actually touching them. As soon as the block is in place, lay a level lengthwise along the block. If it is not level, tap it into perfect position. When it is level from end to end, do the same and level it from side to side.

You can use the handle of the trowel if you prefer, but you can also use a regular carpenter's hammer. One effective way to level a block is to set it gently into the mortar, then push down on one corner to get a level reading. If you cannot push it to the proper point, leave the level in place and push down with one hand and with the other hand tap the end of the block until it is level. Use gentle taps rather than heavy blows.

As soon as the block is perfectly positioned, lay the one that joins it at right angles. See FIG. 6-10. Start by "buttering" the end of the second

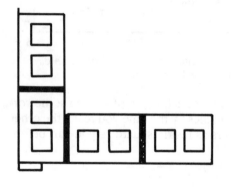

6-10   Butt one block into the first block and mortar it in place. The corner block on the second course laps, or bonds over, the first block, and this pattern will continue to the top of the wall.

block by standing it on end and using the trowel to spread a bead of mortar along the ends. When you set the block into place, ease it forward until the buttered end of the block touches the first block. Then apply enough pressure so that mortar is forced out slightly at the juncture.

Use the same procedures and use the level and pressure until the second block is level. Now, lay three of four blocks in both directions, and then return to the corner and start to build up several partial courses.

When you lay the first block in the second course, the block will reach across the first block and part of the second block in the first course. See FIG. 6-11. This way, you achieve a proper bond. The end of the first block in the second course will be perfectly even with the outside edge of the very first block you laid.

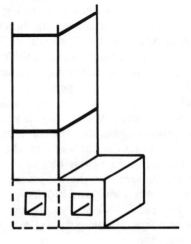

6-11 The dotted line shows how bonding is created. Bonding gives the wall its strength and integrity. Each block should end halfway across the block below it.

As you lay subsequent blocks, stand the block on end, lift a trowel of mortar, and spread the mortar evenly along the ends of the block. To use a trowel effectively, hold it so that your fingers curl around the handle and your thumb extends along the handle and toward the blade. Your thumb will help you to control and balance the mortar-loaded trowel.

To butter a block, lift the loaded trowel and start the point down beside the corner of the block and then slide the trowel along the end of the block so that you scrape the mortar from the trowel onto the block. Do this on both ends of the block, then lift the block and set it in place.

Some masons find that if they use the back of the trowel to press the mortar into the groove when they butter the block, the mortar is not likely to fall out when the block is set into place. A good way to lift a block is to use one hand and hold the thick partition (You have already noted that the partition is much wider on one side than the other, and set the block so that the thick partition is handy) and lift the block. At the same time use your other hand to hold the end of the block that has not been mortared.

By balancing the block, you can set it into position and gently press it forward to compress the mortar joint. Then use the trowel to cut away excess mortar. When all four corners are built as high as they must go, you can start to fill in the remainder of the courses. The height of the corners depends on whether you plan to have a basement or only a crawl space. It also depends on whether you plan to build the complete walls of the house from concrete blocks.

Building codes usually require that 12-inch blocks be used underground. This means that the basement, if you have one, will be made of 12-inch blocks. When you reach the top of the basement walls, you can use 8-inch blocks the rest of the way to the top of the wall.

COMPLETING COURSES

Once corners are laid, stretch a line from one corner to the other. You can use a block line or a nail and a string. If you use the block line, stretch the cord until it is taut and set the block on the corner of the first block in each corner. The block should be high enough that the line is exactly where the top of the blocks in the course ought to be.

As you lay blocks along the line, lay a bed of mortar and then butter and set the blocks into position. Use your level to see that each block is level and true and take a visual reading to see that the block is positioned properly in relation to the line. If you see that one block is higher than the line, push it down until the top is aligned with the line.

Do not let the blocks touch the line and push it out. Hold your level against the sides of the blocks so that the level touches two or three blocks. Be sure that the blocks are firmly against the level. If there is a space between level and blocks, your blocks are out of line.

Lay each block so that the ends of the block fall halfway along the blocks below. Maintain this type of progression along the entire length of the wall line.

Step back occasionally from your work to see if there are problems not clearly visible while you are standing too near the wall. Correct problems while they are still easily managed. Do not let mortar set up until problems are corrected.

JOINTING

Proper bonding means that each block you lay, after the first course, will partially cover two other blocks. If you only stack blocks one on top of the other, even when the mortar hardens, you can dislodge the blocks rather easily, which means that you do not have great strength in the wall to resist pressure, wind, and other destructive forces.

When you work on the second course, make certain that the mortar joints always occur at the center of the block below. Do not let the joints widen to the point that the joint occurs over the cavity of the block.

The mortar joints of the first, third, fifth, seventh, etc., courses should be perfectly parallel. Similarly, the joints of the second, fourth, sixth, eighth, etc., courses should be parallel.

Occasionally, you should hold the level diagonally across the face of the wall to be sure that the joints are meeting properly and to see that the wall is maintaining trueness. Do the same with vertical readings by holding the level straight up and down the wall, and continue to lay it along the blocks to see that you are keeping courses level.

If you notice that mortar joints or bed joints (where blocks join end to end and where one block is laid on top of others) are getting too thick or too thin, make the necessary corrections as quickly as possible. Remember that you will be joining courses from two other walls and you do not want the bed joints to be uneven.

Mix only small batches of mortar until you see how rapidly the work progresses. Use the same method of mixing as that described in the chapter on brick siding. You will find that laying concrete blocks requires a great deal more mortar than brick laying, so when you see that you can move fairly fast with the work, you might want to mix larger amounts of mortar.

If you do not plan to parget the wall when you are finished laying the blocks, you will perhaps want to joint the wall before the mortar dries and sets up. The jointing process works much like jointing bricks. After you have worked for a couple of hours, press your thumb or fingertip into the mortar in one of the first joints you made and see if the concrete has set up enough to "take" the imprint. This means that the mortar is set up enough to allow you to push your fingertip or thumb into the mortar, but the mortar must be hard enough to hold the imprint of your thumb. The surface of the joint should be as consistent as, for instance, a fully baked cake layer.

Stop laying blocks when the mortar has set up enough for you to joint. Then use a jointer (which you can buy at the hardware store) or use the end of a brick or the edge of a 2-×-4 section. Joint by raking the edge of the jointing tool along the vertical joints. Do all of the vertical joints at one time, and when they are all jointed, joint the horizontal joints.

Jointing not only gives a finished, neat, and professional look to the work but also compresses the mortar and pushes it against the blocks on either side of the joint. This compression causes a better seal and prevents moisture from seeping into the joints.

If too much moisture enters a wall, it will seep out through the blocks and cause a discoloration. Often, a dull gray color appears on the block surfaces, and this discoloration is difficult to remove until the wall has dried out completely.

Another problem is that moisture inside the wall can freeze. The freezing causes an expansion, and the wall can be damaged.

REINFORCING AND INSULATING

Check with your local building code about insulation inside a concrete block wall. Learn what type of insulation is needed, if any, and how much of it. You might need to enter the insulation at several points while the wall is low enough for you to install the vermiculite or other insulation easily. Remember that insulation does not prevent heat or cooling loss; all it does is slow down the passage of hot or cold air through the wall. Concrete blocks are very porous and do not supply totally satisfactory insulation. If you fill the blocks with the preferred type of insulation, you ensure greater comfort inside the house and considerable savings in heating and cooling costs.

You can buy insulated cement blocks. These blocks are not only resistant to the passing of heat and cooling but also act as sound-proofing materials. See FIG. 6-12.

Some area building codes require steel reinforcement wire every four or five courses of blocks. You install the wire by laying a mortar bed, just as you would do if you were preparing to lay the next course of blocks, and then lay the wire atop the mortar bed and push it into the mortar until it is embedded well. You can then lay more mortar on top of the wire or lay blocks on top of the wire. The weight of the blocks will press the wire into the mortar and you will secure the necessary bonding strength.

The steel wire comes in long sections (5 or 6 feet long) and 8 inches wide or slightly less. The wire will not show after you lay the course of

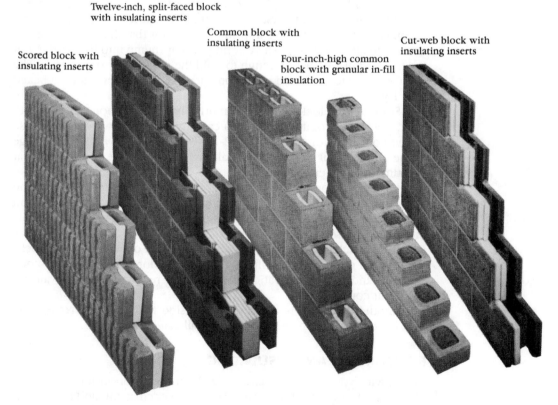

6-12 Builders are increasingly using insulation with masonry. This illustration shows how insulation and masonry can be combined.

blocks. The logic behind the wire is to lock or bond the entire course together.

Lay the wire sections along the entire length of the wall. When you place one section of wire against the previous one, overlap the ends by 6 inches. When you lay the wire, place it completely around the house perimeter. Every wall must have it.

You can buy wire reinforcement materials from your concrete supplier. Some areas do not require wire, so check to see if you need it, then act accordingly.

BREAKING AND CUTTING BLOCKS

Almost without exception, you will find that occasionally you will need to break or cut a block. This usually arises when you are completing a course of work and need a half block in the center of the course.

You can cut a block in two ways. First, there is a special blade for a circular saw that will cut a concrete block smoothly and quickly. Unfortunately, the blades are expensive, they wear away quickly if used often, and the cutting process creates a great deal of dust. You must also have a source of electrical power.

You can buy the blades at most hardware stores, and you install them just as you would any other blade. When you cut concrete blocks, it is absolutely essential that you wear protective glasses and gloves. Long sleeves are highly important. A mask to keep you from breathing the dust is also important. The dust erupts in clouds of particles and inhaling these can be bad for your lungs.

Cut a block by marking the cut line clearly, then setting the saw in position. Lift the back of the saw slightly so that you are not cutting through the entire side of the block at one time. It seems to work better if you cut a thin groove, then return and cut along the groove a second time, and finally cutting it all the way through.

The advantages to using a circular saw are that you get a straight, smooth cut each time and you waste virtually no blocks. With the straight and neat cuts, you get a far more professional-looking job. If you are laying blocks in a circle or arch, you will need to make cuts precise, and a circular saw does the job very well.

The second way to cut a block is to use a chisel with a wide blade, one at least an inch at its broadest point. Start by placing the blade of the chisel on the cut line and tapping the butt or end of the chisel sharply with a hammer. Move the blade an inch or so and tap the chisel again. Do this all the way across the cut line, and then turn the block over and make the chisel marks along the cut line on the reverse side.

When you have scored or marked the block adequately, you can hold the chisel in the center of the cut line and strike it with a hammer sharply and the block will break along the scored line. You may have a slightly irregular cut, but it will work in almost any kind of masonry work that a do-it-yourselfer tries.

The final way to get half a block or a portion of one is to break it with a masonry hammer. You can also use an ordinary ball peen hammer or claw hammer. Mark the cut line and strike the block along the cut line several times with the hammer. Do not hit the block hard or you will break it. Keep tapping the block along the line until you hear the sound of the hammer on the concrete suddenly change from a high-pitched clanging sound to a more mellow sound. That sound is your clue that the block is ready to break.

Turn the block over and repeat the process. When the tone of the impact changes to a mellow or dull sound, strike the block on the middle of the cut line and the block will fall in half. You might have an irregular cut line but you can smooth the cut with a chisel or hammer and you can turn the block and use the back side if the cut is better on that side.

You can buy scored blocks that are specially made to be cut with a hammer. These blocks will break easily and exactly in half, and you will not have any waste. If you break an ordinary block, in almost every case, one end will be ruined. See FIG. 6-13.

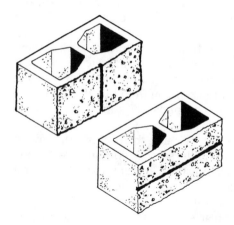

6-13 Scored blocks are exceptionally useful and helpful if you need to use partial blocks. Scored blocks break easily and accurately with little or no waste.

You can cut a block in a variety of shapes. Practice is the best way to learn, just be prepared to ruin several blocks in the process. If you are concerned with saving money, eliminate the need to cut by laying out your wall so that whole blocks can be used whenever possible.

PARGETING

When the concrete block wall is completed, you may want to top it with what is often called cap blocks. These blocks are laid flat and can be bought in thicknesses of 2 to 4 inches. These blocks are solid, and when you cap a wall with them, you have no holes for insects, small animals, or rain to enter.

When the wall is completed, you can leave it the natural color of concrete or you can seal it and paint it. Or, you can parget the wall. This process consists of spreading a layer of smooth mortar over the entire surface so that the finished look resembles stucco or adobe.

To parget a wall, be sure that your mortar is elastic and moist enough to spread well and cling to the wall. Remember that if you plan to parget, do not joint the wall. Instead, you need to cut the mortar off evenly so that there is no indentation along the surface.

Pargeting holds better if the block wall is slightly damp, so you might want to sprinkle the wall with a hose before you start to apply the parget. When you are ready, use the back of the trowel to scoop up a load of mortar. With an upward arc motion, place the trowel blade against the wall and press inward slightly as you move the trowel upward. The mortar will spread smoothly and evenly.

With each stroke, overlap the previous stroke by 3 or 4 inches. Make regular visual inspections to be sure that you are keeping the parget material at a uniform thickness. Use the trowel to smooth out any obvious irregularities. You will also need to smooth out any trowel marks as you progress.

Try to start the pargeting work while you have plenty of time to cover the entire wall. It is troublesome to try to stop work one day and resume the next day. The older parget is dry and hard and it is extremely difficult to smooth and blend the two surfaces.

If you must stop in mid-wall, feather or thin the final stages of the parget surface until it is paper thin. The next day you can smooth more parget over the dried surface.

WINDOWS AND DOORS

You can buy grooved blocks that are especially designed for use in installing windows in concrete walls. When you reach the point where windows are to be installed, use grooved blocks on both sides of the window opening and be sure the grooves are aligned perfectly.

When the wall is high enough for the windows to be installed, buy the windows (do not buy them until you are ready to install them; they are easily broken and expensive to repair) and hold the entire unit high above the window opening. Align the aluminum or similar type of edge and fit it on both sides into the grooves. Let the window slide gently downward so that the entire unit is held in place by the edges.

You will notice that the lips or flanges of edges are scored at quarter-inch intervals. You can use pliers to twist off any sections of the flange that you do not need.

The reason for the flange is to allow you some room for error or for improperly spaced openings. Remove only what is necessary for the window to fit exactly into the grooves in the blocks. When the window is installed, you can apply mortar into the grooves to hold the window tight and to provide added weatherproofing.

Installing doors in concrete block walls can be difficult unless you use several simple rules or practices. One of the easiest methods is to finish the door frame on the sides before you concern yourself about the door. As you lay blocks install nails, heads inside the blocks, into the wet mortar so that the points of the nails stick outside the door frame.

When you have done this in the mortar joints of every block in the door opening, when you are ready for your door frame you can hold the framing timber against the nails and strike the framing timber with a hammer and drive it onto the nails. In this way you can attach the frame without using steel nails.

If you prefer to use steel nails, you can drive them through the framing timbers and into the blocks. Take great care in using these nails, which are especially designed for use with concrete or other masonry products. These nails are made of steel, not from wire, as typical nails are.

The heads of steel nails will pop off easily if you hit the head at an angle, and the loose head will fly at great speed across the room. Such a projectile could easily inflict serious eye damage. It is almost like firing a low-powered bullet. Be sure to wear eye protection any time you drive steel nails.

INSTALLING LINTELS

If the windows and doors are to be installed in mid-wall (and not reach the top of the wall) you will need to install lintels over the windows and doors. Without lintels, you will have nothing on which to lay the courses of blocks over the openings.

You can buy lintels at hardware stores or concrete products supply companies. Measure window openings and add several inches on each side to get the length for the lintels. You will want 4, 5, or 6 inches of extra metal on each side, which is then laid onto a bed of mortar just as wire reinforcements are laid.

Lay blocks across the opening as you would if there were a solid course of blocks below. You might need mortar bed joints that are slightly thicker than normal so that you will have room for the lintel metal and mortar.

Do this at all window openings and door openings. When you lay blocks across the lintels, you have a strong and well-supported door and window area. If the lintel is recessed slightly back from the outside edges of the wall, you can use mortar in the joints to cover the metal so it will not be seen.

As with all work of this sort, check your local building codes before moving too rapidly. There may be a specific thickness or width required in your area, and it is far better to learn the requirements before you have progressed too far.

FINISHING UP

At the end of each day's work, cover all green or wet masonry work with plastic sheets. Weight these down with blocks or bricks or lengths of wood so the wind will not blow the covering off.

The reason for this added step is to keep an unexpected storm from washing out the mortar joints. Rain can ruin half a day's work in a short time. You can still use the blocks, but your mortar and your time are wasted completely. It is also a good idea to keep concrete and blocks covered and thus protected against weather. Soaking wet blocks cannot be laid with satisfaction.

You can use plywood to cover cubes of blocks, if you have plywood handy. The panels are heavy enough to stay in place and you can cover and uncover the blocks quickly.

When the wall is completed and pargeted, you have built a wall that serves as a type of siding. You can later, if you choose, add brick veneer over the blocks, or you can seal and paint the blocks whatever color you choose. Be sure to seal the blocks. If you don't, they will absorb moisture and paint. You will waste gallons of paint because the paint will seep through the blocks.

On the inside of the completed house, you can leave the blocks and your "siding" will also serve as interior wall covering. Or you can cover the blocks with drywall or paneling or any of the other varieties of wall coverings available.

Chapter 7

Vinyl siding

Vinyl siding is one of the greatest innovations in home construction to be marketed in this century. It manages to incorporate economy, endurance, beauty, *and* ease of installation. It needs little or no maintenance; it can be installed in a short time; and it can be easily taken down and replaced by another siding. Vinyl siding has cut deeply into the aluminum market in the reasonably short time it has been available. It is now making rapid gains on wood and brick as the most popular siding in the nation.

To call the siding *vinyl* might not be totally accurate. It is made up of polyvinyl chloride, better known as PVC. PVC is a plastic compound formed into shape at high temperatures. A member of the thermoplastics group, it can withstand the higher temperatures, unlike polyester resins used in building boat hulls, which cannot be reformed. PVC has the necessary flexibility and impact resistance to meet exterior siding requirements at reasonable cost. Vinyl sidings can vary greatly from one manufacturer to another and even from one grade of product within the same trade label.

Manufacturers state that the secret to PVC is that it is more like wood than ceramics or metals. The vinyl is very flexible, somewhat chemically inert, and a nonconductor of heat and electricity. Finally, its chemical stability keeps it from corroding as many metals do.

In terms of maintenance, outdoor wood surfaces require repainting or refinishing every five to seven years, while vinyl rarely, if ever, needs painting, even when installed. It comes from the manufacturer ready to be used.

Vinyl looks very much like wood from a distance, and even up close, it can be distinguished from wood, if it is installed properly, only with careful scrutiny. The major difference is that the vinyl always looks virtually new rather than weather-beaten. See FIG. 7-1. The ability of vinyl to

7-1 Vinyl siding combines an attractive wood look with efficiency and economy. Note that the trim work of this house adds significantly to its overall attractiveness.

resist weather is legendary. While wood is subject to deterioration by wind, sun, rain, and other powers of nature, vinyl keeps its color, shape, and appearance. See FIG. 7-2.

7-2 Unique styling is combined with vinyl accents for a wall covering that is architecturally beautiful as well as highly weather-resistant.

You can buy vinyl siding that is manufactured in nearly all of the popular styles of traditional wood siding from clapboard to beaded siding to Dutch lap. Before you make a choice, ask the dealer to show you samples of all the designs and styles available. Even better, ask a dealer to refer you to someone local who has installed vinyl siding and then contact these people to learn first-hand how they like their siding and whether they would recommend it to others. See FIG. 7-3.

7-3 Vinyl siding comes in a variety of shades and effects to suit every style house.

One of the major advantages of vinyl is the fact that it looks good on virtually any type of house. You can use different styles of siding for various parts of the house. One style can be used on walls, while a different style is used on dormers and a third style is used on eaves or soffits. Before you invest in various styles, find a house with similar siding and see how well you like the mixture. If you are in doubt, stick with one style.

There is a vinyl siding for virtually every type and style of house. Small houses covered with vinyl look trim and neat. Large houses maintain their appearance of grandeur and beauty. See FIGS. 7-4 and 7-5. Shop around for the best materials for your needs.

7-4 This house is an example of how siding can blend with the age and decor of a house.

7-5 Siding can restore historic houses to their original splendor. Siding comes in a number of colors and can usually accurately reflect an age or era.

ESTIMATING MATERIALS

You can help the dealer (and yourself) by knowing roughly how much siding and materials you will need. To get an accurate measurement for materials, first measure the length and height of all walls and multiply the two dimensions to get the number of surface square feet you will need to cover. Do this with all walls.

If you plan to install siding at the ends of the house where there is a roof peak, measure the lower part of the house as if it were a square or rectangle and figure the square footage. Then, measure the distance from the peak of the house to the top of the first floor and then multiply the distance by the width of the house. Divide this number by two.

For example, if the house is 20 feet wide and the distance from the peak to the top of the wall is 9 feet, multiply the two numbers. The result is 180 square feet. Because the peak area forms a triangle, you cannot use the area of a square. Take half of the 180 square feet and the result is 90 square feet. Add the 90 square feet to the area of the rectangle or square formed by the bottom part of the house.

If you have a gambrel roof, consider the middle part of the end of the house as a square or rectangle. You will have three small triangles left over. Treat each triangle as a square to get the surface area, then divide each triangle by half. When you are finished, add the square footage of the large rectangle and the areas of the three small triangles plus the square footage of the major part of the house.

To measure dormers, treat one side of the dormer as a square and multiply the length times the height. Do not divide by two. Use the total figure to take into account the other side of the dormer. Use the same principle for the front of the dormer as that used to measure the peak of the house.

To measure for eaves or soffits, multiply length by width as you would for any rectangle. When you buy the siding, be sure to purchase the J-channel and F-channel materials. These materials provide the finished look for the soffit.

No matter how well you plan and how carefully you figure, there will inevitably be waste. In fact, even professional building contractors assume a 10 percent waste on house framing and construction. If you don't want to build in the extra percentage, you can include doors and windows in all of your measurements. The siding not needed to cover these wall openings will possibly be enough to offset any waste.

MATERIALS AND TOOLS

There are several items you'll need to have at your fingertips before you begin installing the siding. You will need sawhorses or saw bucks with boards or plywood spread across them; a circular saw with appropriate blade; good heavy-duty scissors or snips; a hammer; line level; framing square; pencil; measuring tape 25 feet long; and nails designed for siding installation. See FIG. 7-6.

7-6 Do not try to work with vinyl on the ground. Use sawhorses or tables to keep siding from breaking or bending.

If you have access to a nail hole punch and a snap lock punch, you'll find that these can be very handy additions to your toolbox. The nail hole punch creates elongated holes in the cut edge of a panel. If you need to trim a panel, you can punch new nail holes easily and quickly. See FIG. 7-9.

The snap lock punch is similar except that it punches tabs in the panel that has been trimmed. The trimmed edge is lock punched to provide a finishing course at the wall tops of window bottoms.

You will also need some type or elevated work surface. You can rent or buy scaffolding, ladders, or aluminum planks. Ladders are the cheapest but least efficient means of climbing to the top of a wall. They are unsafe, awkward to move, and must be moved each time you need to work a few feet away. You need a work surface that will allow you to walk up and down to do all the nailing and fitting of an entire section of wall. See FIG. 7-7. The type of nails usually recommended are 8d galvanized box nails. Ask your dealer for the proper nails to use for the siding you have chosen.

7-7 If you are installing siding over existing walls, cover the wall with sheathing.

INSTALLATION

If the existing siding on the house is in bad shape, you might need to remove the old before installing the new. Don't install siding over decayed or badly damaged wood siding. If you can keep the old siding, go over the wall surface and drive in all nails that have worked their way loose. These protruding nail heads can damage siding and create unsightly irregularities.

Start your work in a place that is not as noticeable as other parts of the house. Choose a back wall, for instance, or a side wall that is not as clearly visible from the road or highway or by neighbors. You are not at all likely to create an untidy job, but it makes sense to do your experimenting where it counts less. Your greatest challenges will come at corners or where siding meets posts or soffits. Read installation instructions carefully and make sure that you have all of the necessary materials. The only difficulty you are likely to encounter when installing siding will be where the window framing fits over the window sill area and in corners.

Leveling the wall

The first order of business is to ensure that your wall is level and plumb before any sheathing or starter strips are placed. Begin by measuring carefully. The old carpenter's adage is to measure twice and cut once. The sider's motto might be to measure over and over until there can be no possibility of a mistake. If the wall is not square, that is, if it is not perfectly symmetrical at corners, each with a 90-degree angle, you must make immediate adjustments rather than wait until the wall is nearly completed to try to deal with the gaping holes or uneven panels.

Measure from corner to corner of the wall. Measure at the top, at the bottom, and in the middle. If the wall is not plumb, there might be a discrepancy that needs modifying. Measure from top to bottom at both ends of the wall.

Use a line level to be certain that you are starting with a level starter strip. The reason is significant: if your first panels are not level, the top of the wall will have ill-fitting panels that result in a long expanse of uncovered wall.

If the wall is highly irregular, you might need to use furring strips before you install siding. If you apply the siding to an uneven wall, the siding will have a wavy appearance that greatly detracts from the overall attractiveness of the house.

To install furring strips, use 1-×-3 strips spaced vertically 12 inches on center. If necessary, use shims to bring the nailing surface into a vertical trueness. Install shims under the end of the furring strip that is recessed too much or that tends to lean inward. Use a level to see how far from vertical the wall is. If the wall is 2 inches off vertical, use a 2-inch shim to bring the furring strip out to the proper vertical position.

Nail rigid sheathing to the furring strips. Do not install furring strips over the applied sheathing.

Installing sheathing

When you are confident that your wall is level, install the sheathing or special underlay material that your dealer recommended. You can buy a variety of sheathing designed for use with vinyl siding, and this can be installed quickly and easily. Be sure that your sheathing is rigid. You cannot apply vinyl siding directly to studding. The surface of the sheathing should be as flat as you can possibly get it.

Some products come from the carton folded like homemade fans. In this case, have a helper hold one end of the strip while you move to the other end of the wall and unfold the sheathing as you walk. If the section is longer than you need, you can cut it with a pocketknife or razor knife.

Use the sheathing nails recommended by your dealer to attach the sheathing to the wall. You will need to put three or four nails in the first end, then, while a helper holds the strip in place, move toward the free end, nailing at the top and bottom. Be sure that the entire length of the covering is supported well along the length of the wall.

Before you start to install the siding, nail up the covering as far as you can reach. You might need to install only one width of the material before you start to nail up siding panels. If you don't want to set up scaffolding unnecessarily, start hanging siding panels as soon as the one width is in place. But first, you need to establish a starting point and install the starter strip.

Installing the starter strip

Before you can install the starter strip, you must establish a baseline. You can use your line level to get a proper starting point or you can measure from the soffit to the top of the foundation wall. Either way, the most important step is to be certain that you have exactly the same distance from the bottom edge of the soffit to the top of the foundation wall. If the distance is not precise, you might be able to adjust for a fraction of an inch or so.

Assume that the distance on one end is 8 feet and 6 inches. Mark the point where the first panel of siding will be installed. This mark will represent where the bottom of the panel will rest. Go to the other end, and measure down the exact distance you marked on the other end—8 feet and 6 inches. Now, stretch a line level between the two marks to see if the wall is level at the starting point. If it is not, you might have to adjust slightly for the starter strip.

Next, use a chalk line to mark the level line between the two marks. If you have a helper, have him hold the end of the chalk line at one end of the wall and you carry the line to the other mark. Stretch the line tight, and with one hand, hold the line tight against the wall. With the other hand, reach out as far as you can and pull the line up and then release it so that it snaps back in place sharply leaving a clear chalk line from one mark to the other.

If you are working alone, drive a nail partway in at each of the marks and loop the chalk line over one nail. Take the line to the other nail and wrap it several times after pulling the line taut. Go to the middle of the wall and hold the line firmly in place while you snap the first half of the wall length. Then switch hands and snap the other half of the line.

If you try to snap the entire line at one time, the line might sag, resulting in an incorrect marking. The shorter the distance, the better your chance of getting a perfect reading. A long line tends to bounce, leaving several marks.

Once you have a level starting point, you can install the special starter strip. Let a helper hold one end so that the top of the strip is perfectly aligned with the chalk line. Hold the rest of the strip in place and nail it so that the strip is perfectly parallel to the chalk line, which in turn, is perfectly parallel with the bottom of the soffit or eave of the wall. See FIG. 7-8.

If you do not have a helper, drive a series of nails across the wall exactly along the chalk line. You can then rest the starter strip on the nails while you work. Use 6d galvanized nails unless your dealer has a special recommendation or unless the manufacturer specifically mentions a certain nail. You should be aware that some manufacturers will not guarantee their product unless the proper nail is used in the installation. Do not jeopardize the future of the work because of an inappropriate nail.

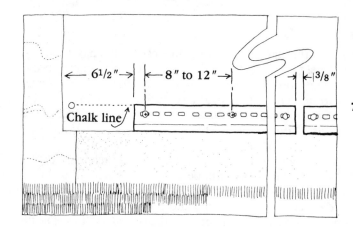

7-8 Install a starter strip at the wall line—the point where the wall framing and the foundation wall meet.

The starter strip might have slots where you need to nail, and the strip should be nailed to the studding under the sheathing. It is a good idea to locate studs and mark them so you know that the nails reach a solid surface. See FIG. 7-9.

You might want to check the level of the starter strip after you have finished nailing. Lay a level along the top of the strip to be sure you did not inadvertently install the strip inaccurately. When you are finished, you are ready for one of two tasks.

Installing corners

Corners are installed much the same as starter strips. Corner units are fitted over the existing surface and nailed in place using the nail slots provided. Unless otherwise instructed, use 6d galvanized nails. Always follow the manufacturer's directions when in doubt, however. See FIG. 7-10.

If you need to cut the corner units, you can do so with a circular saw equipped with a smooth-cutting blade. There are several blades made especially for use with vinyls and similar materials. If a circular saw is not available, you can use a hacksaw for cutting. The hacksaw is slower but the cut is smooth and accurate if you do not try to rush the job.

7-9 Use the nail slots for attaching the starter strips. Be sure to use the nails recommended by the dealer or the siding manufacturer.

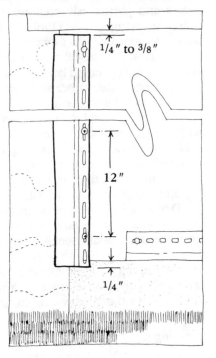

7-10 Install corner posts as shown. These posts will be used to hold the ends of the siding panels.

Lay the unit on the work area so you can hold it securely while sawing. You can allow the unwanted end of the unit to hang over a 2×4 laid at right angles to the vinyl. The flexibility of siding can make it difficult to cut only one panel at a time, so you might want to cut two or three panels at once.

Another helpful suggestion is to elevate the back of the saw so that the blade barely reaches through to the bottom edge of the panel. Advance the saw blade slowly, and don't get in a hurry. If you saw too fast, you run the danger of gnawing the edges, causing the siding to bend so that an incorrect cut results.

You can use tin snips to make short cuts. Snips cut through vinyl very easily and leave a clean cut. Don't try to cut too big a bite at one time. Advance the snips only 2 inches at a time. Slip the vinyl far back into the jaws of the snips so that you are cutting at the shallow part of the snips rather than at the end of the blades.

To rip-cut a vinyl panel, lay the panel flat and use the blade of a square as a guide. Then use a very sharp knife blade, such as a hawkbill knife or razor knife, and pull the blade along the blade of the square as you exert medium pressure. If the blade does not penetrate all the way through the panel, bend the panel back and forth until the vinyl snaps.

When the unit is cut, use galvanized nails to install it. Do this at both corners of the wall. You can buy extra-wide corner posts if you prefer these to the traditional widths. The wider posts work well with larger houses and particularly well with unusually high walls. A two-story house, for example, often looks better with wider corner posts, but you can use standard widths as well.

When you are installing corner posts, if you must use two pieces, be sure to let the top length lap over the bottom one. If you allow the bottom to lap, moisture can gather at the lap and make its way into the siding and decay the wood underneath.

With some vinyl siding products, there is a staggered, double-nail hem for strips and posts. The slots in the hems are about an inch in length and are spaced about a half inch apart, so you have an abundance of nailing possibilities. The double or extra series of slots overlap the first slots in the hem so that there is actually no place on the hem that you cannot find an appropriate place to nail.

Depending on the type of product you are installing and the length of the wall, you might need to install vertical strips between the corners. If this is the case, install them just as you did the starter strip and the corner posts.

Your siding package should contain pre-finished, 8-foot corner strips to be used with all inside corners. You can cut these to the needed lengths and install them before you begin nailing up the siding.

Installing the panels

Before you can install your first course of siding, you will need to deal with the mounting strip on the back of the siding. This strip fits over the edge of the starter strip. In most cases, the siding is not fastened at the bottom. At the top of the first course are nail slots. Drive nails into studding after first placing the nails inside the slots. This holds the siding to the house. See FIG. 7-11. You can use one nail at each stud if you wish. Some siding experts use a minimum of nails, but this practice is to save time and nails rather than for a utilitarian purpose.

7-11 Attach the bottom of the first panel to the starter strip and then fasten the top of the panel to the wall.

At this point, the first course or panel should be resting on the starter strip, which, in addition to supporting the panel, acts as a watershed. The bottom of the panel is supported by the starter strip and the top of the panel is nailed to the studding. When you are nailing in siding, start in the center and work your way out both sides. Do not allow the siding to sag while you are working. Remember, the siding actually hangs from the nails; the nails do not fasten the siding to the walls of the house. Do not nail tightly. Allow the siding room to expand and contract as the temperatures rise and fall. Nails should be about 16 inches apart.

The end of the panel must be fitted into the corner post. You can slip the panel end under the corner post so that there is no way for water or insects to find their way under the siding. You will need to cut the end of the siding at an angle so that the siding will fold neatly over the wood framing. You can cut vinyl with scissors or shears.

Siding is often butt-joined without any type of holder other than the supports on the strips. The second course is attached to the first course by means of an interlocking return leg. The top of the second course is again nailed to the studding. Continue installing the panels to the top of the wall. Be sure to check the level.

It is important to lap siding so that the visible part of the lap is away from the most traveled areas. If you are working to each side of a front walk, the lap should face away from the walk so that it will be less visible. Lap from the front to back of the house so that persons standing at the front corners of the house will not see the laps as well.

Once you reach the top of the wall where the siding joins the soffit, you will need to install special inside corner molding to cover the place where the two join.

Siding soffits, eaves, gables, and dormers

Soffit areas must be ventilated every several feet so that the soffit will not suffer from too much heat or trapped moisture under the siding. You might have seen siding installers simply use a hammer to knock a hole in the existing soffit. The finished hole is large enough to put your fist through. You can accomplish the same ends without resorting to such untidy measures. Drill a 1-inch hole in the soffit and then use a keyhole saw to finish cutting out a small rectangle. See FIG. 7-12.

7-12 Molding is installed where the wall and soffit meet. This trim keeps weather and insects outside.

When you install siding over the soffit, cut short lengths of vinyl and install these at right angles to the wall siding. When soffits are completely covered, you can use inside corner strips where the soffit joins the house. These corner strips will seal the joints and keep out moisture and pests. See FIG. 7-13.

7-13 Soffit and fascia siding units attach easily to existing materials.

If you have dormers, cover these in the same way you did the walls of the house. Cut siding to proper length and angle and use an inside corner strip along the roofline and another at the soffit or eave of the dormer. You can run the siding horizontally or vertically depending on the size and structure of the dormer. Cover gable, eave, or soffit areas not in line with the roofline as if each one is a separate soffit or gable. See FIGS. 7-14, 7-15, and 7-16.

The best and easiest way to fit panels under gables or eaves is to use a large piece of cardboard or a width of scrap wood to use for a pattern. You can hold the cardboard or other surface so that the edges are perfectly vertical. Position the cardboard so that it rests against the eaves or roofline and then draw a mark along the roofline onto the cardboard.

If you held the cardboard straight, your line should give you the same slant as that of the eaves or gable slope. Cut the cardboard and then lay the pattern on a panel of vinyl. Draw the cutline and then cut the panel along the line. Your panel should then fit well under the gable or eave.

You can also make a pattern by snapping a short length of siding into a J-channel and marking a second piece held in position. With the short length locked in place, hold the second length so that the top point of the panel butts into the J-channel along the slope. Mark along the top of the second piece so that the pencil mark is left on the short piece that was locked onto the J-channel. Cut along the line and the short piece can then be used to serve as a pattern.

You can also lock a short pattern piece of siding into the J-channel and use a framing square to indicate the cutline. Hold the square so that the blade extends downward and the tongue extends parallel to the ground. Use the top of the tongue as a guide and mark the short pattern piece.

7-14 and 7-15   These illustrations show how gable or dormer trim is installed. Use the same installation techniques used for the soffit and fascia.

After you have marked the pattern piece and cut it, you'll find that one of the two pieces can serve as a pattern for horizontal siding and the other cutline can serve as a pattern for vertical siding.

The larger length of cardboard used as a pattern will work for a cutline, but you might find that you need to turn the pattern over to get the accurate cut you need. The smaller length can serve as a pattern for any

7-16 Dormer and gable siding is installed in the same manner as walls. The major difference is that each panel is angle-cut on one or both ends.

vertical siding. You can use the same side of the cardboard for the vertical cut.

You might find that the slope of the eave or roofline varies slightly as you move along the gable or eave. In this case, hold the pattern up to the eave or soffit frequently to maintain a perfectly accurate cutline.

When you are installing the siding, slip the cut end so that it fits into the J-channel properly. Lock the panel into the previous panel of siding and nail the panel into place.

Siding around windows and doors

Special window surrounds are available from the same source where you bought your siding. These surrounds are specially formed to fit over the existing window framing. These surrounds are easy to install simply by setting them in place and nailing them. See FIG. 7-17. Drip caps for windows are included as part of the window surrounds or framing. These ensure that there is no danger of rain seeping behind the siding and damaging the wood under the siding. See FIG. 7-18.

When you need to cut a panel to fit under a window, hold the panel in place and mark at both sides of the window. Then measure to see how deep the cut must be. Leave room for expansion, so add 1/16 inch to each side of the cut. Rather than risk wasting siding, use a piece of cardboard or stiff paper as a pattern. Try several cuts until you are certain you have the right one. Then lay the pattern over the siding and cut along the pattern cuts. You will have a neat fit and there will be no waste.

Use the same techniques to install door fittings. When you are install-

7-17 Window trim is secured with smaller nails. Cut the trim so that the fit is neat and waste is minimized.

7-18 Window surrounds or framings are used to seal windows against leaks. When surrounds and drip caps are installed properly, the watershed action diverts water from the joints.

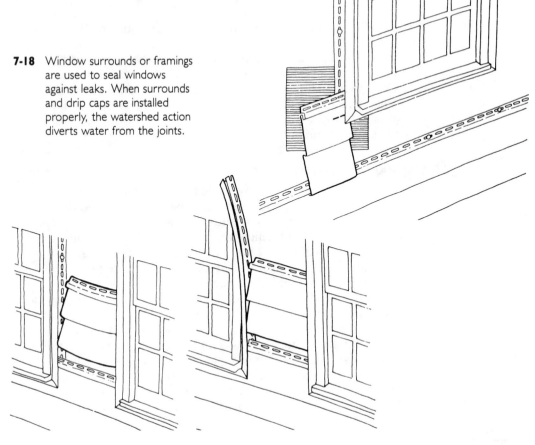

ing door and window trim, use J-channels. Let the J-channel extend beyond the window frame by the width of the J-channel itself. You will interlock these pieces and you will need the extra length.

Chapter 8 offers suggestions on installing vertical siding.

Chapter **8**

Vertical siding

*A*s mentioned in chapter 7, you can use differ-
ent styles of siding for various parts of the house. One style can be used
on walls, while a different style is used on dormers and a third style is
used on eaves or soffits. Vertical siding is one such different and attractive
style.

ESTIMATING MATERIALS

You can estimate how much siding you'll need for vertical siding installations using the formula given in chapter 7.

MATERIALS AND TOOLS

There are several items you'll need to have at your fingertips before you
begin installing the siding. You will need sawhorses or saw bucks with
boards or plywood spread across them; a circular saw with appropriate
blade; good heavy-duty scissors or snips; a hammer; line level; framing
square; pencil; measuring tape 25 feet long; and nails designed for siding
installation.

   If you have access to a nail hole punch and a snap lock punch, you'll
find that these can be very handy additions to your toolbox. The nail hole
punch creates elongated holes in the cut edge of a panel. If you need to
trim a panel, you can punch new nail holes easily and quickly. The snap
lock punch is similar except that it punches tabs in the panel that has been
trimmed. The trimmed edge is lock punched to provide a finishing course
at the wall tops of window bottoms.

   You will also need some type of elevated work surface. You can rent
or buy scaffolding, ladders, or aluminum planks. Ladders are the cheapest
but least efficient means of climbing to the top of a wall. They are unsafe,
awkward to move, and must be moved each time you need to work a few

feet away. You need a work surface that will allow you to walk up and down to do all the nailing and fitting of an entire section of wall. The type of nails usually recommended are 8d galvanized box nails. Ask your dealer for the proper nails to use for the siding you have chosen.

INSTALLATION

Just as with installing horizontal siding, you need to clear the wall area of all obstructions. Drive in all nail heads that have worked loose and install furring strips if the wall is not plumb or vertical. Refer to chapter 7 on checking the wall for level. These same requirements are necessary when installing vertical siding, with one major exception or addition. When you install vertical siding, you **must** install horizontal furring strips. These are attached to the studding, and must be done before you sheathe the house.

Installing furring strips

Siding is never installed directly over furring strips. There must be a smooth, rigid, and level surface beneath the siding. Otherwise, you'll warp, puncture, or twist the siding and create an unsightly finished job. Therefore, furring strips are installed before you sheathe the house.

If you will be installing siding over new construction, install the furring strips after the house is framed. Use 1×3s nailed into position at 12 inches on center. You can expand the distance between furring strips to as much as 16 inches if you must, but don't do this unless necessary.

If you are installing siding over an existing wall, install rigid foam sheathing over the wall. If you don't have a level surface, nail in shims to bring the incorrect area level or into position.

If the siding is to be installed over brick, concrete blocks, or clapboard siding, use furring strips to level the wall surface. Then install the sheathing over the furring strips.

Establishing a baseline

Your next step is to mark a baseline to serve as your starting point for the siding. There are two ways of establishing a baseline. The first is to use a line level held at the wall line—the point where the wall meets the foundation wall. Drive a nail partway into the existing siding at one corner. Locate the nail an inch or so above the wall line. Loop the line level cord over the nail, and carry the other end of the cord to the opposite corner of the house. See FIG. 8-1.

Keep the line taut and have a helper direct you to raise or lower the end of the line until you get a level reading on the line level. If the level reading occurs with the line on or very near the wall line, you are in good shape with the baseline.

The second method for establishing a baseline is using a chalk line for the line level. Just attach the level onto the chalk line and loop one end

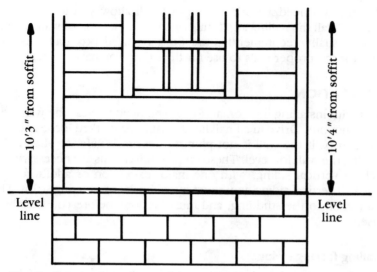

8-1   Getting a level start is one of the most important steps in installing siding. Strike a chalk line along the wall line, but drop 1 inch below the line
to keep moisture out.

over the nail at the corner and carry the chalk container to the other corner. Keep the line level near you if you are working alone so you can tell
when the reading is right. If you have a helper, leave the level in the middle of the wall. When the reading is correct, mark the two points where
the cord was held. Then just remove the line level and chalk the baseline.

Installing corner posts

Before you begin to install corner posts, first check to see that all corners
are straight and plumb. If they are level, position the outside corner post
by laying it against the outside corner and nailing it in place. Nails should
be 12 inches apart. Don't leave nails loose enough so that siding can move
freely but don't drive them in so tight that the siding is not allowed the
freedom to expand or contract with heat and cold. See FIG. 8-2.

Be sure that any overlapping occurs from top to bottom. The bottom
part of any exterior construction should never lap over the top because
that position will allow moisture to seep into the wood area under the siding. See FIG. 8-3.

Install the inside corner post as you did the outside corner. Place the
post material in position and attach it to the strip. Use two lengths of
J-channel in place of an inside corner post if you want. Turn one length
of J-channel so that the short end of the J is backed against the short end
of the J in the other section. The long ends of the Js will frame a right
angle. See FIG. 8-4.

Seen another way, the long side of the first J-channel will be against
the wall on one side of the corner. The long side of the other J-channel
will be against the opposite wall.

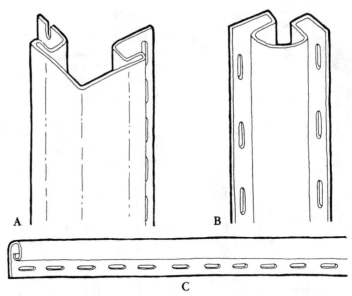

8-2 A) Outside corner post (box post). B) Inside corner post. C) Utility trim. Install the corner post and the utility trim before you try to install the panels. The ends of the panels must fasten into the corner post.

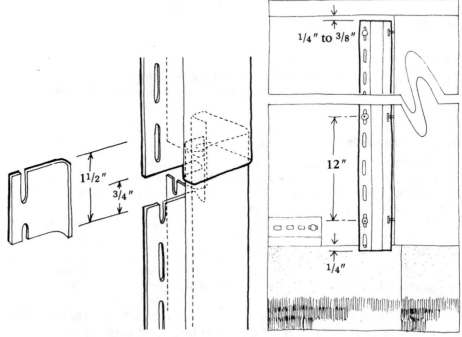

8-3 Use a level to install corner posts. Note that posts are always overlapped with the top section lapping over the bottom section.

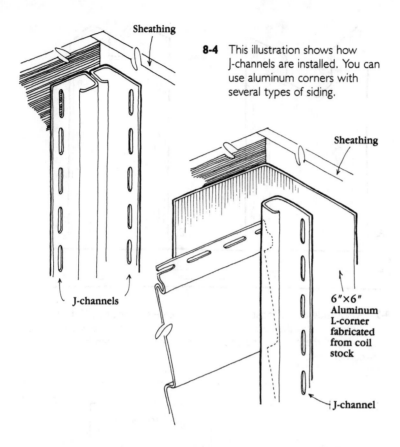

8-4 This illustration shows how J-channels are installed. You can use aluminum corners with several types of siding.

Starter strips are not used for vertical siding. A starter strip will cause the bottom of the siding to curve outward and create an unattractive finished job.

Installing J-channels

J-channels can be installed in two ways, depending on whether the siding will be installed horizontally or vertically. For horizontal siding, J-channels are installed at the ends of the wall. For a vertical installation, the J-channels are installed at the top and bottom of the wall.

When you install the J-channels, allow the two units to overlap an inch or two. The purpose of the bottom and top J-channels is to receive and hold in place the siding. See FIG. 8-5. In order to overlap the two J-channels, you must clip out a section of the nailing flange, about an inch or slightly more. When the small section is cut out, the two channels will easily overlap.

You will need to install the J-channels in an inverted fashion at the top of the wall, similar to the way you installed the inside corner post. A J-channel must also be installed under the soffit so that the short part of the J curve is hanging downward. Nail this unit to the soffit. See FIG. 8-6.

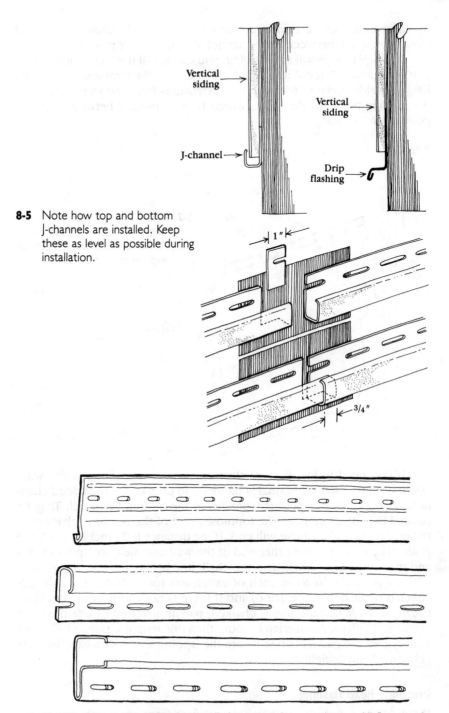

8-5 Note how top and bottom J-channels are installed. Keep these as level as possible during installation.

8-6 Use starter strips for installation convenience and ease. All first panels will fasten to the strips. From top to bottom: starter strip, J-channel, and F-channel.

Again, overlap the J-channels at the top of the wall. Allow 1/4 inch of expansion space between the J-channel and the corner post. See FIG. 8-7.

If you plan to install soffit siding, you can install the F-channels before you begin to install the siding. The F-channel is, as the term implies, shaped like an upside-down F, with the two extensions from the stem serving as the holding point for the soffit, which is then inserted between the two points. See FIG. 8-6.

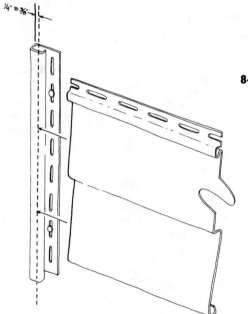

8-7 This illustration shows how panels fit into J-channels. Remember to allow 1/4 inch of expansion room.

If you need to install more than one course of siding on the wall, you'll need to install additional J-channels. To prepare for the added channels, snap a chalk line perfectly parallel to the bottom J-channel. To get a parallel line, measure from the topmost point of the bottom J-channel to the point where the course will end. If the distance is 94 inches, mark the point. Then move to the other end of the wall and measure up 94 inches and mark the point. Then snap the chalk line between the two points.

Always allow 1/4 to 1/2 inch of expansion room. When the siding is affected by heat, it can expand, and if there is not room, some buckling might occur. When the line is chalked, nail an inverted or upside-down J-channel in place. An overlap of more than one length is needed. Cut out 1 inch from the nailing flange where the lapping will occur. Nail the next J-channel in an upright manner.

Installing head flashing

Head flashing, a device to prevent moisture from seeping between the joint units, must be installed between channels. Head flashing is angled so that one part of the flashing is flat against the wall and under the upper channel. The flashing then angles out so that it separates the two channels and then curves or angles downward.

Rain or other moisture would have to penetrate between the two channels, then be forced upward past the end of the flashing. Any water that seeps between the flashing will be diverted downward and drip harmlessly to the ground.

Installing panels

Before you even began to install vertical panels or nail anything, you need to first find the center of the wall. Measure to the exact center of the wall between the two corners, but don't measure from top to bottom. Mark the exact center at the top and again at the bottom. Use a chalk line to snap a mark down the wall, from top to bottom, exactly halfway from corner to corner. Now, measure from the line to the corner on each side of the line. This measurement from the mark to the corner will determine whether you can use whole siding panels.

Siding experts insist that for the best appearance, you should have the same number of panels on each side of the center of the wall. If whole panels will not fit, plan to trim both end panels to create a perfect fit. For example, if you have 9 inches too much siding for the entire wall area, plan to trim $4^1/2$ inches from two panels. This leaves the same trimmed space on each corner, balancing the wall exactly.

Be careful not to cut off the nailing hem when trimming. Trim from the other edge, then use furring strips to compensate for the loss of the locking channel. Install the two trimmed panels so they fit into the corner post. Nail these in place. Do this on both ends of the wall.

When the corner trim work is done, install the full panels to cover the remainder of the wall. Remember that if you need to lap, do it so that the top materials lap over the bottom to prevent infiltration of moisture.

At the corner where the furring must be installed, slip the furring strips inside the channel at the outside corner post. Then fasten the furring strip to the rigid insulation and studding under the sheathing. See FIG. 8-8. Next, slide the cut edge of the panel into the utility trim. There are snap locks that must be fitted together, so be sure these are engaged.

When you are installing vertical vinyl siding, remember that the principles don't differ in any important sense from installing horizontal siding. Seen another way, simply imagine that the wall has been turned so that the left corner is now the top and the right corner is now the bottom. Each panel will fit into the corner posts, and you can then nail the free end to the framing of the house. The next panel will fit into the last one installed, and the free end is nailed. Follow this progression all the way across the wall.

When you need to overlap panels, note the factory precut notches. When you overlap, let the overlapping section extend no farther than half the length of the precut notch. See FIGS. 8-9 and 8-10.

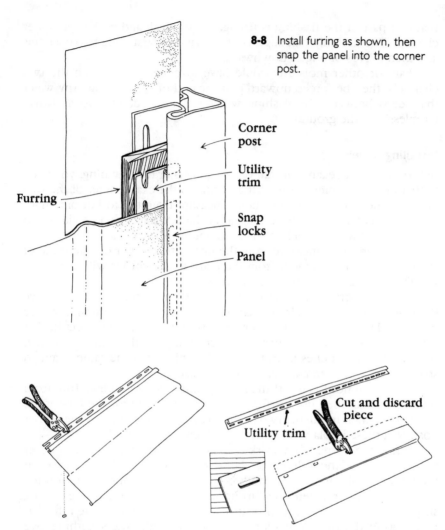

8-8 Install furring as shown, then snap the panel into the corner post.

Corner post

Utility trim

Furring

Snap locks

Panel

Cut and discard piece

Utility trim

8-9 A nail hole punch and a snap lock punch might prove useful in making minor adjustments.

Siding soffits, eaves, gables, and dormers

Siding installed around soffits, eaves, gables, and dormers, as well as windows and doors, will, of course, need to be cut. One of the easiest ways to cut siding is to use a circular saw with a fine-tooth blade. The flexibility of siding can make it difficult to cut only one panel at a time, so you might want to cut two or three panels at once. Another helpful suggestion is to elevate the back of the saw so that the blade barely reaches through to the bottom edge of the panel. Advance the saw blade slowly, and don't get in a hurry. If you saw too fast, you run the danger of gnawing the edges, causing the siding to bend so that an incorrect cut results.

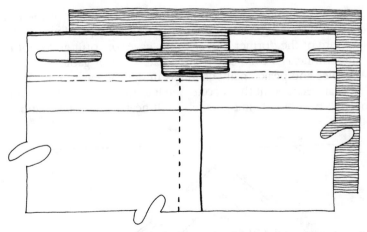

8-10 When lapping panels, let the lap section (the panel that fits on top of the first panel) point away from the line of traffic so the seams or laps are not readily apparent.

If a circular saw is not available, you can use a hacksaw. The cutting will go slower, but if you are patient, a hacksaw will do the job. You can also use tin snips to make short cuts. Snips cut through vinyl easily and leave a clean cut. Don't try to cut too big a bite at one time, though. Advance the snips only 2 inches at a time. Slip the vinyl far back into the jaws of the snips so that you are cutting at the shallow part of the snips rather than at the end of the blades.

To rip-cut a vinyl panel, lay the panel flat and use the blade of a square as a guide. Then use a very sharp knife blade, such as a hawkbill knife or razor knife, and pull the blade along the blade of the square as you exert medium pressure. If the blade does not penetrate all the way through the panel, bend the panel back and forth until the vinyl snaps.

If there are louvers or ventilation slits in the gable, don't cover these; ventilation is necessary. Attics can become incredibly hot during summer months and the intense heat can cause damage to materials stored in the attic and even contribute to the spontaneous combustion that sometimes occurs.

When you are installing siding over a soffit, you'll need to provide for ventilation. If the soffit is not already ventilated, cut a small hole, large enough for an air passage, and install the louvered or ventilated panels over the hole. Without this ventilation, the soffit will overheat and buckling can occur.

Usually, soffit panels run at right angles to the wall, and you will need to cut short lengths of vinyl. Trim the soffit panels with the trim pieces included with your siding. When soffits are completely covered, you can use inside corner strips where the soffit joins the house. These corner strips will seal the joints and keep out moisture and pests.

If you have dormers, cover these in the same way you did the walls of the house. Cut siding to proper length and angle and use an inside corner strip along the roofline and another at the soffit or eave of the dormer. You can run the siding horizontally or vertically depending on the size and structure of the dormer. Cover gable, eave, or soffit areas not in line with the roofline as if each one is a separate soffit or gable.

At gables and peaks, nail J-channels under the eave or soffit. Nail in the first channel, then fit the second one into the end of the first one. You will need to trim or cut siding panels to fit neatly into the J-channels. See FIG. 8-11.

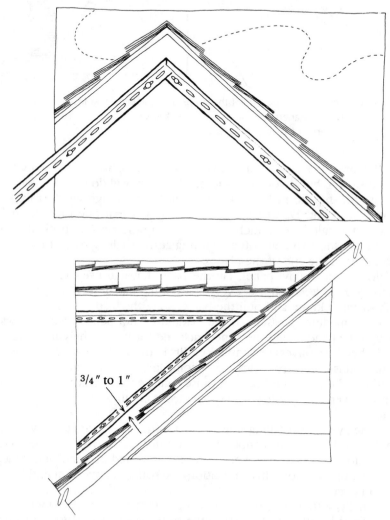

8-11 When installing siding on gables, install the trim along the roofline as shown. Cut a pattern to use when you need to cut panels to fit the slope of the roof.

The best and easiest way to fit panels under gables or eaves is to use a large piece of cardboard or a width of scrap wood to use for a pattern.

You can hold the cardboard or other surface so that the edges are perfectly vertical. Position the cardboard so that it rests against the eaves or roofline and then draw a mark along the roofline onto the cardboard.

If you held the cardboard straight, your line should give you the same slant as that of the eaves or gable slope. Cut the cardboard and then lay the pattern on a panel of vinyl. Draw the cutline and then cut the panel along the line. Your panel should then fit well under the gable or eave.

You can also make a pattern by snapping a short length of siding into a J-channel and marking a second piece held in position. With the short length locked in place, hold the second length so that the top point of the panel butts into the J-channel along the slope. Mark along the top of the second piece so that the pencil mark is left on the short piece that was locked onto the J-channel. Cut along the line and the short piece can then be used to serve as a pattern. See FIG. 8-12.

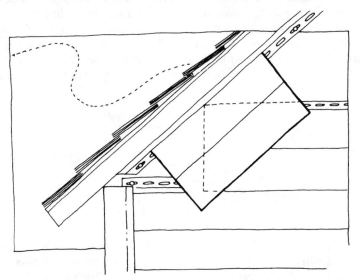

8-12 This illustration shows how to cut the slope's angle pattern with ease. Check the fit, because the roof slope might not be uniform in all places.

You can also lock a short pattern piece of siding into the J-channel and use a framing square to indicate the cutline. Hold the square so that the blade extends downward and the tongue extends parallel to the ground. Use the top of the tongue as a guide and mark the short pattern piece.

After you have marked the pattern piece and cut it, you'll find that one of the two pieces can serve as a pattern for horizontal siding and the other cutline can serve as a pattern for vertical siding.

The larger length of cardboard used as a pattern will work for a cutline, but you might find that you need to turn the pattern over to get the accurate cut you need. The smaller length can serve as a pattern for any vertical siding. You can use the same side of the cardboard for the vertical cut.

You might find that the slope of the eave or roof line varies slightly as you move along the gable or eave. In this case, hold the pattern up to the eave or soffit frequently to maintain a perfectly accurate cutline.

When you are installing the siding, slip the cut end so that it fits into the J-channel properly. Lock the panel into the previous panel of siding and nail the panel into place.

Siding around windows and doors

Special window surrounds are available from the same source where you bought your siding. These surrounds are specially formed to fit over the existing window framing. These surrounds are easy to install simply by setting them in place and nailing them. Drip caps for windows are included as part of the window surrounds or framing. These ensure that rain does not seep behind the siding, damaging the wood under the siding.

When installing siding around windows, install J-channels first so that the window is completely surrounded. You can square-cut the ends of the J-channels or miter-cut them. Square cutting is easier but miter cutting is neater. Be sure to lap where necessary. Do not butt-join the channels. See FIG. 8-13.

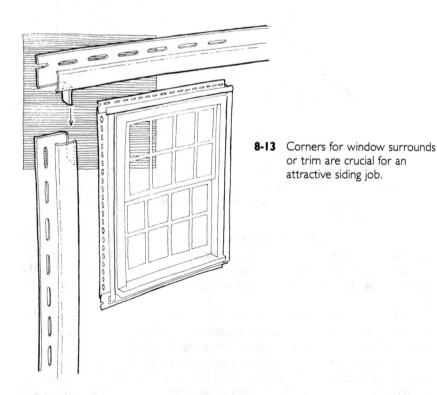

8-13 Corners for window surrounds or trim are crucial for an attractive siding job.

Install the top and bottom J-channels first. When these are nailed into place, measure and cut the side channels. When you are ready to join these, make cuts in the bottom of the channels and bend the tab downward so that the side channels fit under the tabs for a tight fit. See FIG. 8-14.

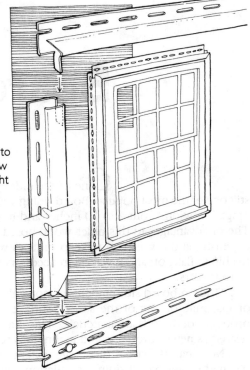

8-14 This illustration shows how to miter the corners of window surrounds or trim. You might want to practice with short lengths of waste material before you try to trim windows.

When you are finished with the wall, including the soffit, gable, eave, dormer, windows, and doors, move to another wall. If the job is completed, you are ready to apply sealants where needed and to paint, provided you feel that another color is necessary. One of the advantages of installing vinyl siding is the freedom from maintenance. Try to use colors that are compatible with your exterior decorations rather than paint. If you use a siding that requires paint, refer to chapter 13 on siding accessories.

$Chapter$ **9**

Board siding

One of the oldest forms of house siding is also still one of the most popular. Board siding was once long wood boards that ranged in width from 4 to 10 inches and in thickness from 1 to 2 inches. The disadvantages to this older wood board siding are that the wood was expensive and it was hard to keep surfaces well painted. The paint tended to chip or flake off and it was often necessary to paint the siding every three or four years.

Modern board siding includes not only wood boards but hardboard or masonite or any of the several surface materials composed of wood products or blends of materials. The major disadvantages have disappeared as newer products and techniques reached the market.

New paints have, to a large extent, solved many problems that plagued earlier wood siding installations. Pressed wood or similar products often do not need painting except after installation. Many of these surfaces are factory-primed and ready for the final coating of paint. There are also many effective sealers on the market that fight decay and insects. Weather-proofing paints or coatings to keep moisture out of the materials are also available.

The advantages to board siding are numerous. The surface of the finished siding is neat and attractive; there is little warp or bending; the materials are very easy to install; the cost is very affordable; and the life expectancy of the siding is very long; the materials are very easy to work with; and the waste is minimal.

ESTIMATING MATERIALS

When you visit your dealer, be ready to tell him approximately how much siding you will need. You can get a fairly close estimate by measuring square or rectangular walls from corner to corner and from top to bottom and multiplying the distance in feet. If a wall is 10 feet high and 40 feet long, multiply the two distances and you get 400 square feet. Your dealer can then tell you how much siding you need.

When you are measuring gables, remember to measure the width of the gable at its widest point and then measure the highest point and multiply the two distances. Then take half the square footage indicated. If a gable is 10 feet high and 30 feet long, when you multiply you get 300 square feet, but your gable is a triangle and, therefore, you need only half of that amount, so add 150 square feet to the square or rectangular product of the wall area.

When you measure, do not subtract the square footage of doors and windows. You will have some waste, and the siding that was included as part of the window and door covering will make up for any waste.

TOOLS AND MATERIALS

The first steps in nearly all do-it-yourself carpentry projects are to prepare the surface and assemble the tools and materials that you'll need. To install board siding, you will need a rule or measuring tape; a framing or carpenter's square; hammer; circular saw or good handsaw; scaffolding or ladders to permit you to work at higher levels of the wall; sawhorses or sawbucks; chalk line; and your siding materials.

PREPARING THE SURFACE

How the surface is prepared depends on several aspects. If you are working on a new building, you need do nothing more than complete the sheathing work. If you are remodeling or re-siding an older building, you will need to remove the present siding surfaces. Unlike vinyl and several other siding materials, board siding is not installed over existing siding.

If the building already has siding, remove the surface material carefully. Remember that old siding is a favorite nesting place for wasps and hornets and other biting or stinging insects. If the building is extremely old, you might expect to encounter a variety of life inside the walls. Work carefully. Use gloves and eye protection as you work. It is also a good idea to wear long-sleeved shirts and full-length trousers. It is not unusual to find snakes and mice, even rats, inside the walls.

Remove old siding with a crowbar, if you have one, or a hammer with a good strong handle. Start at the top and remove the top course of siding. Then work your way down the wall. If the old siding is wood, you will have nails to handle. Be very careful. Rusty nails can inflict painful and potentially serious wounds that might require medical attention.

If you are working on a scaffold, take care to pass old siding down as you remove it. Have a helper stack the siding away from the work area so there will be no danger that someone will step on a nail and receive a painful foot injury. You also have the danger of tripping over the siding.

If you are working alone, when you remove a length of siding toss it several feet away from the scaffolding. Do not drop it near the scaffold because of the danger of falling over it or stepping on it as you descend from the scaffold.

To remove old wood siding, the first step is to remove all molding where the wall meets the soffit. You might also want to remove the corner boards before you start to take down the old siding. To remove siding, slip the blade of the crowbar or wrecking bar under the edge of the siding lap—the bottom edge—and pry upward. The nails will give slightly and easily. Pry at several places until all of the nails within reach are nearly out of the wood.

Do not try to pull the board off the wall with a strong jerking motion. The board might break and splinters can render injuries. The board might also bend or bow as the nails resist your pulling, and when the nails pull free suddenly, the board snaps loose and can cause injury.

If the nails are longer than usual, use a thin fulcrum under the crowbar. A short length of 1 × 4 works well. If you are using a hammer, use the fulcrum regularly to prevent damaging the hammer handle.

Remove window framing also as you work, unless you intend to keep the old framing. If you have trouble removing these boards, you can pry the board partially free and then strike the board with a hammer. Do not hit the nails but strike near the nails. The result will be that the board will snap back in position and the nails will be loosened so that they extend an inch or so from the board surface. At this point, you can use the crowbar or hammer to remove the nails. This technique also works well with siding boards.

When you are removing old aluminum siding or damaged vinyl siding, you can take down the molding and corner boards first, then the window framing or molding. Then use a claw hammer to remove the small nails from the nail apron or slots. When the nails are removed, use the crowbar to slip the curbed end of the blade behind the siding and pull it away from the wall. You can then unsnap the siding from the course below it. Continue this way until all of the siding is removed, including the starter strip at the bottom of the wall.

You can remove most other sidings by using a crowbar and hammer. If you do not intend to use the materials elsewhere, such as in a small utility building or tool shed, rip the siding from the wall and move it a safe distance from the work area. When the wall is completely freed of old siding, check the sheathing to see that it is acceptable.

Many older houses do not have sheathing. If you find no sheathing, you might need to add the cost and time of sheathing installation to your work schedule. You can buy rigid foam panels that add greatly to the insulation of the house. These panels are usually 4 feet × 8 feet, a total of 32 square feet, in size. They are lightweight and can be handled easily by one person.

At the corners, you might want to install plywood sheathing. This sheathing not only helps to insulate, it strengthens the wall, particularly at the corners. The result is that the corners stay square and the wall resists warping and sagging. Rigid foam insulation does not strengthen appreciably, but the plywood is one of the strongest materials used in modern building. If you want to use metal bracing instead of plywood, this is fine.

The plywood panels, which are usually the same dimensions as the foam sheathing, are heavy enough that you might need help in installing them. Remember to drive two nails two-thirds of the way into the wall line (where the wall meets the foundation). Lift the plywood panel and rest the bottom of it on the nails. Then maneuver the panel until the edge of the panel is aligned perfectly with the corner post. When the position is correct, nail the plywood in place. Drive nails a foot apart up and down every joint. If your studs are not spaced correctly, you might need to make corrections.

Many, if not most, building panels are manufactured in 4-×-8 dimensions so that they will fit over traditional studding and you will not have to cut them. Studs are usually installed in a 16-inch, on-center manner. This means that the distance from the corner post to a point halfway across the first stud should be 16 inches. From the midpoint of that stud to the next one should also be 16 inches. From the outside of the corner post to the midpoint of the fourth stud should be exactly 48 inches.

The position of the two middle studs is not crucially important. If they are an inch or two out of place, no harm is done. The position of the fourth stud is highly important. If it is not in the precise location, the end of the plywood panel will not have a nailing surface behind it.

When you encounter such problems, it is usually much easier to add a new 2-×-4 stud than it is to remove one and renail it in a different location. When you remove a stud, you are likely to split or break the ends and weaken it too much for use. If the fourth stud is only an inch or so off center, you can nail the extra 2-×-4 stud to the existing one. If the spacing is very bad, leave the old stud in place and install another one in the proper place.

When you encounter a stud that has bowed because of excessive weight or because it was installed while still green, remove the stud and replace it. You want to have the wall surface as smooth and level as you can possibly get it.

INSTALLATION

It is highly important to get off to a good start. This means that your first course must be installed so that it is perfectly level. There are three ways to get off to a level start. You can use a line level, a chalk line, or a rule or measuring tape. It is recommended that you use all three, particularly if you are a novice at installing siding.

Use the line level at the wall line. If you have a helper, have him or her stand at one corner of the wall and hold the cord that holds the line level at the wall line. Take the other end of the line to the far corner and hold it at the wall line. You will need to have the line pulled tight and the line level near enough for you to read it accurately. See FIG. 9-1.

If the bubble is not centered between the lines of the level, raise or lower the end of the line slightly. You might need to adjust both ends of the line until you have a perfect reading. Locate the lowest point of the

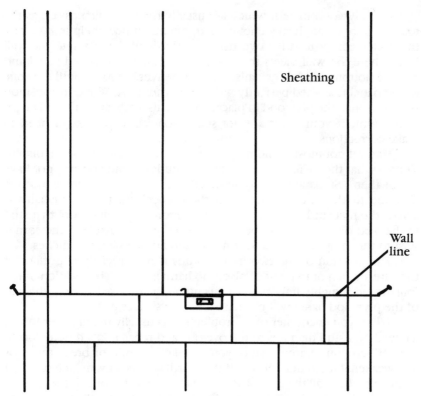

Sheathing

Wall
line

9-1 Use a line level to get the correct chalk mark for the wall line. Let the siding fall
an inch or so below the wall line.

wall line and take your level reading from that point. In other words, do
not let the level line occur above the wall line. If you do, the result will be
an unsightly product and the exposed wall line will admit moisture and
insects. When the proper level is reached, mark the line location on both
ends, and use a chalk line to mark the level line across the wall. When you
use a chalk line over a long distance, do not try to mark the entire line at
one time.

While someone holds one end of the line, tie the other end of the
line around a nail shank and then to the midpoint of the wall and press
one finger tightly against the line. As you are facing the wall, hold the line
against the wall with your right hand. With your left hand, reach as far as
you can toward the corner and lift the line carefully and pull it until the
line is stretched so that when you release it, it will snap against the wall
and leave a clearly visible mark. Then hold the line in place with your left
hand and reach as far as you can with your right hand and snap the other
end of the line.

If you try to mark the entire line with one snap, the line will most
likely sag or bounce off the wall and leave several marks. You need to have
only one perfectly level and clearly defined line.

You can eliminate one step by attaching the line level to a chalk line.

When the reading is correct, hold the line against the wall and snap as before. Do not let the line level move freely. Remove it before you snap the line.

If you are working alone, you can drive a nail at the proper locations and loop the end of the line around one nail and then stretch the line until you can tie it around the other nail. Proceed as before when the line is secure.

The third step is to measure from the soffit (which is the bottom of the eaves of a house) to the chalked line. See FIG. 9-2. The distance should be the same at each end of the wall. If there is a minor discrepancy (of an inch or so) you can correct the problem by making very small adjustments of the location of the wood siding courses. If the problem is great, you will need to modify the location of the chalk line or you will need to make a special cut for the top course.

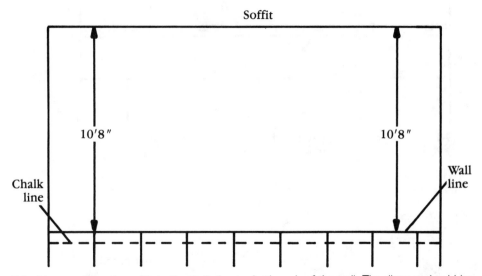

9-2 Measure from the soffit to the chalk line on both ends of the wall. The distance should be exactly the same, if possible. You can make corrections if the discrepancy is small, but it is better to start with the same measurements.

Once the starter line is established, you can install the starter strip. This strip is a narrow and straight length of wood (usually a 1×2) that is installed along the chalk line to provide a proper watershed. If the board is installed flat against the wall, water will run over the board and down the foundation wall. If there is a watershed strip used, the water will drip off the edge of the board and not run down the foundation.

Many foundation walls are not sealed properly and the water is absorbed by the porous surface of the foundation wall, eventually seeping under the house or into the basement. The water will also discolor the wall.

When the starter strip is installed, and the corner boards are installed, you are ready to nail the first course in place. You can drive several nails partway into the wall so that the shank of the nail is against the starter strip. When you position the first course, the bottom of the first board should be even with the bottom of the starter strip. See FIG. 9-3.

You can nail the first course at the top, about an inch from the top edge, so that the nails go through the siding and the sheathing and into the studs and the corner post. See FIG. 9-4. You can now mark the second course line or you can pause to make a story pole to use when you install later courses.

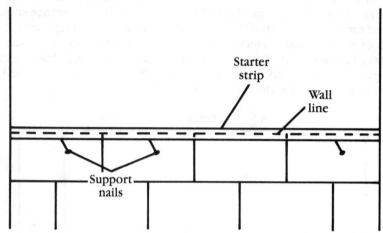

9-3   Install your starter strip so that the bottom of the strip falls slightly below the wall line. If you are using vertical boards, omit the starter strip.

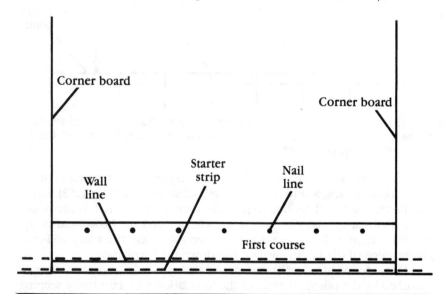

9-4   When you nail up the first course of boards, drive nails through the board and into the studding. Keep the nails near the top of the board so that nails don't show.

A story pole is simply another way of double- and triple-checking course levels. By using this simple device, you can guard against getting the courses out of alignment. Taking a very basic precaution like this can save you time, money, and worry in later stages of the siding.

MAKING A STORY POLE

All you need to make a story pole is a rule or measuring tape, a long board, and a pencil. The device itself is used to let you constantly check whether you are staying on schedule with your work.

Assume that you are using 6-inch boards with 4 inches to the weather. This means that your boards are nominally 6 inches wide. That is the width before the finishing work was done. The final board will be 5^1/2 inches wide. The 4 inches to the weather refers to the space that will be visible as you stand and look at the wall. It is also the space that will be exposed to rain, sun, wind, and other natural forces. The rest of the board will be lapped by the next course.

If your wall is 10 feet high, you will need to cover 120 inches. If you discount the lap space, your boards will be only 4 inches wide. This means that you will need 30 whole boards to reach the top.

When you make the story pole, stand a long board or 2 × 4 against the wall. You can hold the bottom end of the timber so that it is perfectly even with the bottom of the first course. Make sure that the board will not hit the soffit.

Take the board down and mark it every 4 inches. Use a square to get the mark straight. As you use the story pole, each new course will end at a mark. If you need to do so, number the spaces between the marks according to the course level. The numbers will show which course you are installing.

Use the story pole in conjunction with other methods of keeping proper alignment. These double checks take only a few seconds, but they are very important, particularly as you are getting started. You can clamp the story pole to the corner post to keep from having to move it repeatedly, but you will need one for each corner post. See FIG. 9-5.

After the first course is installed, measure up 4 inches from the bottom and mark the location. Do this on both ends. Or, you can mark down from the top. If the board is 5^1/2 inches wide, you will need to mark down exactly 1^1/2 inches.

When the board is marked, stretch your chalk line between the two marks and strike a line. If you need to do so, drive three or four nails partway into the first board. Let the point of the nail start on the chalk line. Use small nails and pull them out when the course is installed.

Hold the board into position and let it rest on the nails. Drive nails into the upper edge of the board and into the studding. When the course is nailed securely, pull out the holding nails. The chalk line and the nail holes will not be visible.

After you have installed two or three courses, measure from the soffit to the top of the last board installed from time to time. Do this at both

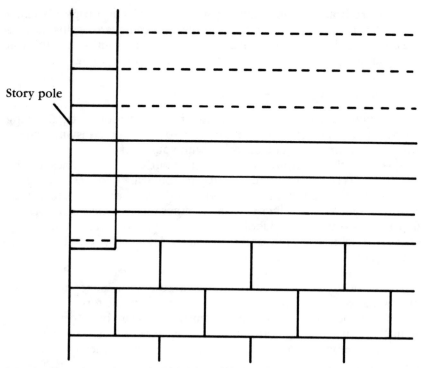

9-5 A story pole can be used with brick and block masonry as well as with clapboard siding. Mark the board and then nail or clamp it to the corner. You can also stand it on the ground, provided you have a correct measurement from the wall line to the ground.

ends. If the distance is the same or very nearly the same, you know that your level is correct.

Hold the story pole up to the corners after each course or so. Be sure that the bottom is level with the bottom of the first course. Then compare the mark on the story pole with the top of the last course installed. The marks should be even.

To help you to hold the story pole accurately, nail a 1-inch strip, about 6 inches long, across the bottom edge of the story pole. If you nail the strip to the actual bottom of the story pole, when you hold the story pole against the wall, fit the strip under the edge of the first course and pull upward to keep the pole tightly in place. This avoids the danger of letting the story pole slip or slightly drop.

You can also locate a resting point for the end of the story pole. Use a concrete block or similar resting point that will not move or wobble as you measure. If the ground slopes slightly, you might need to alter the height of the block at the other end of the wall.

It is generally more accurate to use the strip at the bottom of the story pole. You can feel the pressure against the bottom of the first course and not have to worry about the correct height of the resting place atop the block. Your story pole need not be 10 feet long. You can use one that is only 3 or 4 feet long. Just move the story pole up as the wall climbs.

Remember that with each course, you will need to perform four basic steps. First, measure and chalk the line for the next course. Second, measure from the soffit to the top of the course. Third, drive in the holding nails to rest the next board on. Fourth, after the board is nailed enough to hold it in place, use the story pole to check the spacing before you do the final nailing.

COMPLETING THE WALL

Depending on the type of siding you are using, you will need to set up a story pole to fit the different widths of the siding boards, whether they are masonite, hardboard, or other wood. If you are using 9-inch boards, leave 8 inches to the weather and mark off $1^1/2$ inches. For 8-inch boards, leave 6 inches to the weather. For 12-inch boards, leave 10 inches to the weather.

When you are cutting boards, use a circular saw with a fine-toothed blade. A carbide-tipped blade will last longer and keep its edge longer than the common blade. Some materials, such as wood, will splinter slightly on the top side when cut with a circular saw. You can eliminate the problem by marking and cutting from the bottom side. If you are using a handsaw, the wood boards will split slightly on the bottom side, so you can mark and cut from the top side.

If you are uncertain how to cut the materials you are using, use a small scrap or cut the very end off a longer length of the siding. If the cut is a good, usable one, mark and make all of your cuts from that side of the siding.

When you come to windows and doors, install the framing around the opening and butt the ends of the siding into the framing. Do not try to install framing over lap siding.

When you are fitting around the bottom or tops of windows or other wall openings, it is good if you can use a length of siding that does not have to be cut. If you cannot install full-width lengths, measure the amount to be cut off. Write down the measurements and then mark and cut the siding piece.

It is easier for some people to hold the siding in place and mark it against the window or door frame. If this method works best for you, continue to use it. When you are cutting out for fitting around a window frame, don't forget to include the lap space in your calculations. See FIG. 9-6.

You can strike a chalk line completely across the window and its frame if you need to do so to keep your courses level and evenly spaced. The chalk wipes away with little difficulty. You can use this continuous chalk line to check for alignment or you can measure from soffit to the top of the course on both sides of the door or window. You can also use the story pole to verify that you are maintaining correct alignment.

When you are ready to install the final course, if you have measured correctly, you will have, under the best of conditions, a space left that is

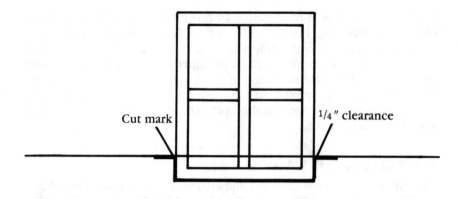

Cut mark   1/4 " clearance

9-6 When you reach the bottom of windows, mark the board and cut out the necessary section so that the board fits snugly over the window opening. Allow 1/4-inch clearance.

equal to the width of the siding you are using. If you are using 6-inch siding and you have only a 4-inch space left, you can mark, chalk, and rip-cut a length of siding to fit snugly into the space.

It might work out that, despite your careful calculations and plans, you have gotten one end of the siding out of proper alignment. If you are off by an inch or so, measure the space left between the top course and the bottom of the soffit. Measure at both ends of the wall, if the siding reaches all the way. If the siding does not reach from corner to corner, measure to the point that the siding reaches. Measure the space. If one end of the siding must be five inches and the other only four, lay the siding face up, and then mark the two points and strike a chalk line from one end to the other and rip the siding along the line. You can later install molding to cover the points where the soffit and the siding meet. The molding will cover any slight or trivial discrepancy created when the piece was cut.

If you stayed close to the top when you nailed the siding to the studding, you will not have any nails showing. One of the most unsightly aspects of siding installation is nail heads not only visible but exposed to weather and rusting or allowing rust-stained water to discolor the siding itself.

When all the siding on the wall is installed, go to the next wall and repeat the processes of removing the old siding, preparing the wall surface, and measuring and striking the wall line markings before you install the starter strip. Follow the same steps on the remainder of that wall and any other remaining walls.

Before you start subsequent walls, check to be sure that no nails or nail heads protrude far enough to cause trouble. Drive in any nails that are not seated fully.

GABLES

When installing siding under gabled roofs, you will encounter slanted roof lines and eaves and soffits. You will need to angle-cut all pieces that fit against the soffit or eaves. It can be difficult to find exactly the right angles, but there are at least two ways of handling the problem.

One way is to strike a chalk line, using the line level for accuracy, all the way to the point where the siding meets the eave or soffit. Mark the siding length for the top and bottom. If the siding is 5½ inches wide, strike the lines exactly 5½ inches apart. Then measure the distance along the top line and then along the bottom line. When you are ready to cut the siding, you'll find that the bottom side of the siding is several inches longer than the top. See FIG. 9-7.

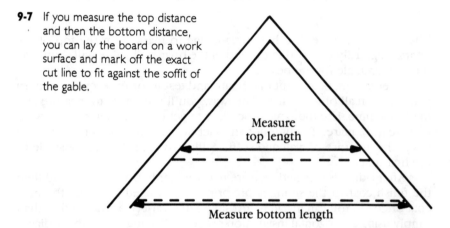

9-7 If you measure the top distance and then the bottom distance, you can lay the board on a work surface and mark off the exact cut line to fit against the soffit of the gable.

Measure top length

Measure bottom length

Lay out a length of siding to prepare it for the angle-cut. Measure the siding for the two lines. Then use a square or other straight edge to get the cut line. When you make the cut, hold the siding in place to see that the fit is good.

If it is, save the angle you cut off and use it for your patterns for all future cuts on that side of the gable. When you are ready to make the next cut, lay the piece that was cut off so that it is aligned with the end of the siding board. Mark along the angle formed by the pattern piece.

A second way to get an accurate cut is to hold a level at the eave and locate the vertical position, then mark along the inside edge of the level for several inches. Measure down the line until you locate the space that corresponds with the width of the siding board. If the siding is 9½ inches wide, measure down that distance. See FIG. 9-8. Then measure from the line to the eave or soffit.

When you get ready to cut the angle, mark it as follows: If the distance from the line to the eave is 5 inches, measure over 5 inches from the end of the siding and mark a light line across the board with a square.

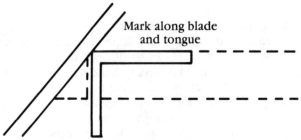

9-8 To get the correct pattern for future cuts, hold the square as shown and mark across the board. Next, measure from the edge of the blade to the soffit. Mark the point and then use the square to mark from the bottom point to the top point.

Then use the square or other straightedge to mark from the top of the board diagonally outward to the end of the board. The line will show you the proper angle for the best fit.

After you mark and cut one board and test it for fit, keep the pattern and use it on all other boards. This way, you'll only have to measure and mark one time. Use the same procedure to get correct angles for all walls that are not square. If a cut is not an exact fit, remember that molding will cover the juncture of wall and soffit. Still, strive for the best possible fit the first time.

After siding is installed, you are ready to apply primer paint and then the finish coat. If the siding is pre-primed, you need add only the final coat or coats. You can install board siding in a variety of ways rather than simply using a horizontal installation process. You might find that a diago-

9-9 After boards are installed, double check to see that all boards conform to the side of the house. If any are bowed, nail through the board and into the studding. If you must work on a ladder, be certain that the ladder is firmly positioned.

nal installation fits your house well. See FIG. 9-9. You can also install diagonal siding in more than one direction.

The next chapter, chapter 10, covers a long-standing favorite siding of Americans everywhere—log siding and log kits.

Chapter 10

Log siding

*A*fter centuries of use, one of the oldest building materials in western civilization is making a strong comeback. In recent decades, more and more homebuilders and home owners have found that log houses or traditional houses with log siding a welcome alternative to brick, board, or vinyl siding for houses.

For decades, most people thought of a log house as a one-room cabin in the forest, far removed from the comforts of modern construction as well as from the necessities of electricity, waste disposal, city water, and neighbors. In recent years, log houses or frame houses with log siding have been constructed in both rural and urban areas, and the log house or the log-appearance house has become a rather common sight.

The log exterior or the log-walled house has come to symbolize the American frontier in pre-Revolutionary days, but in truth, the log cabin is not American in origin. The first known log houses were built in Scandinavian countries. Neither were the log houses always one-room cabins with few comforts; some had as many as five stories and contained more than 5,000 square feet of heated space.

On the American scene, the log cabin was often built as a last resort. It was a house to be endured until something better could be constructed. That "something better" was a house framed with milled lumber. Only in the past 20 years has the log cabin been regarded as a desirable permanent house that is easily heated, maintained, repaired, and decorated.

It is also true that log houses or log-sided houses were not economical to build. Decades ago, a log house that cost $15,000 to build contained only $1,000 worth of logs. Only one-fifteenth of the total construction cost of the house went for the logs.

Log structures were also very time-consuming to build, and the basic materials were so heavy that it was almost impossible for one person to construct anything larger than a basic cabin. Such houses were difficult to insulate and insect-proof. They tended to be cold, drafty, and expensive to maintain.

Modern log houses or log-sided houses are the total opposite. Such houses are neat, tight, comfortable, and a welcome addition to nearly any type of neighborhood. See FIGS. 10-1 and 10-2. The interior of these log homes can also be very modern and as comfortable and roomy as the inside of more contemporary homes. See FIG. 10-3.

10-1   Log siding can present a true log-cabin look, and the ends of log siding units can be manufactured to look like complete logs.

10-2   Note that siding goes all the way to the peak of the roof, and joints are not visible anywhere. The workmanship is neat and the house is strong and tight.

10-3 Logs can function as both exterior siding and interior wall coverings. You can use squared logs or studded wall framing covered by tongue-and-groove wall covering.

One of the major reasons homebuilders turned to logs was for the same reason logs fell into disfavor: heating and cooling. Because log houses could not be chinked and weather-proofed easily, they were not popular a century or two ago. Today, because wood is one of the best insulation materials available, log houses are now considered economical to cool and heat.

Four inches of solid wood reportedly possesses more insulating value than a concrete wall 5 feet thick. New vinyl chinking and more accurate methods of cutting and fitting logs have eliminated an enormous percentage of the heating and cooling loss, and many log or log-sided houses are extremely easy to heat or cool.

In mild weather, no heating or cooling is needed inside a typical log house, even when daytime temperatures rise as high as 90 degrees or when nighttime temperatures drop to freezing. A well-chinked log house remains comfortably cool even in summer, except in the very hottest weather, and a medium-sized woodstove alone can heat a 3,000 square foot log house adequately when the temperature regularly falls to the 30-degree or lower mark at night.

Log siding first appeared as a commercially feasible building material around 1936. At that time, log siding was cut manually and costs were high because production was extremely slow. With the advent of the power saw, production is much faster and costs have dropped somewhat.

If you want the look of logs without having the cost, weight, and energy-consuming work of logs, you might find that log siding is worth your consideration. You can buy log siding or you can cut your own, provided you have access to good, straight trees. You will also find that the cost of these materials can be shockingly expensive or amazingly economical, depending on the route you choose. As a rule, the more work you are willing to do, the lower your cost will be.

THE ECONOMICS OF LOG SIDING

If you are looking for an inexpensive siding, log siding is not the choice. Log siding is expensive. In fact, it is among the more expensive of the forest products. If your only consideration is aesthetic, however, log siding is an excellent choice.

While it is often pointless to discuss costs because of the constantly fluctuating expense of building materials, a brief comparative cost of log siding versus traditional siding might be helpful. In 1991, the cost of white pine log siding, 7 inches wide or slightly wider, was $1.50 per foot. Cedar log siding was $2.10 per foot for the same size. A 4-×-8-foot panel of exterior plywood will cover 32 square feet of wall space for about $20. To cover 32 square feet of wall space with white pine or cedar log siding will cost several times as much as plywood.

If you are set on having log siding but the cost is a deterrent, consider cutting your own siding, provided you have access to trees at a reasonable price. The work is rather laborious and time-consuming, but the economics can be rewarding. You can cut your own at a cost of less than 10 cents per foot, which is far better than $1.50 or $2.10. If you must buy the trees, the cost becomes considerably greater. This option is discussed later in this chapter.

INSTALLATION

Log siding can be installed over old siding if need be. You can install log siding over old wood, plywood, or even over concrete blocks and other masonry surfaces. You will need to install furring to provide a smooth and even nailing surface.

Rather than use 1-×-3 furring strips, you might want to use larger lumber for the log siding, such as 1×4s or 5¹/₄×4s. Thicker furring strips require longer and larger nails, so consult a dealer before installing the log siding.

One method of installing log siding is to install the furring strips with adequate nails and then nail the log siding directly into the furring strips as you would nail up wide boards. Do not use a starter strip. You do not want a watershed type of wall structure. Ask your dealer what size and type of nail is needed for the product you buy.

When you are nailing up furring strips over masonry surfaces, you will need to use steel masonry nails. Never use steel nails unless you are wearing protective glasses. The heads of these nails can break and fly across the room with astonishing speed and force. You can easily lose an eye if you are struck in the face by one of these rather lethal projectiles.

When you are driving steel or masonry nails, do not try to hit the nail as hard as you would hit an ordinary wire nail. Try to hit the nail squarely on the head with soft and regular taps that are sufficient to drive the nail into the masonry. If you strike the nail at an angle, the head will break off. Be sure to bring the head of the hammer down straight on the nail.

Install the furring strips horizontally every 12 inches or so. The nails should be long enough to penetrate the masonry by at least 1$1/2$ inches.

One slower and more expensive way to install furring is to use anchors and long screws. You will need to drill holes in the log siding at each end, two holes per end. The holes must be slightly smaller than the shank of the screws. You can use a masonry drill bit and, while holding the siding in place, let the bit bite into the masonry slightly at both locations and on both ends. Take down the siding and then drill the hole into the masonry where the two marks on each end appear. Then insert a plastic anchor to receive the screw. Hold the siding back up and install the screws.

The advantage of screws over nails is that if the log siding contains excessive moisture, the fibers of the wood will shrink and the nails will become loose in the holes when the siding dries. Nails can also be pulled out of masonry. Screws are strong and threaded. The fluted shank of screws hold inside the plastic and the siding will remain securely fastened.

In all cases, consult with the dealer who provided the siding. Follow his instructions whenever they vary with installation information you receive from other sources.

When you install log siding, except for corner boards, proceed essentially as you would with other types of board siding. You have two options. You can butt the siding into the corners, or you can buy log siding with simulated whole-log appearance. The end of the log creates the illusion of whole, rounded logs only at the corners. These rounded ends can be joined in a number of ways.

Some log siding suppliers suggest 2-×-6 studding rather than conventional 2-×-4 framing. See FIGS. 10-4 and 10-5. You have the option of

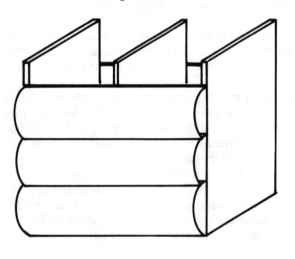

10-4 This illustration shows how log siding fits against wall framing. Normally, 2-×-6 studding is used rather than traditional 2-×-4 studding.

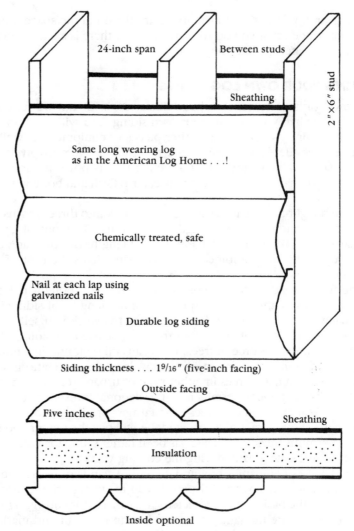

24-inch span

Between studs

Sheathing

2"×6" stud

Same long wearing log
as in the American Log Home . . .!

Chemically treated, safe

Nail at each lap using
galvanized nails

Durable log siding

Siding thickness . . . 1⁹/₁₆" (five-inch facing)

Outside facing

Five inches

Sheathing

Insulation

Inside optional

10-5 A sectional view of a log-sided wall. The log effect can be used on both sides of the wall framing and then the center of the wall filled with insulation.

installing interior wall coverings that are also made of log siding. Any insulation can be installed between the two surfaces as shown in FIG. 10-5.

Furring strips create a dead air space between the log siding and the concrete block wall. This space adds to the insulation properties of the wall. Dead air is one of the very best methods of insulating, which is one of the reasons for using commercial insulation.

Manufactured insulation is filled with air spaces that prevent or retard the passage of heat or cooling through the spaces. When you compress traditional insulation, it loses a large amount of its insulating capability. The dead air space then acts as a barrier to prevent the passage of heated or cooled air. If you wish, you can install insulation in the space, but it is not recommended that you do so, particularly if there is a likelihood that moisture can penetrate into the spaces.

CUTTING YOUR OWN LOG SIDING

If you own, or have access to, a good chain saw with a powerful engine and fairly long bar, you can cut your own siding. You will need, in addition to the chain saw, only a few other pieces of equipment as well as a source of trees. Be fully aware of the potential dangers involved with using a chain saw. Remember that anything that is powerful and sharp enough to rip dense wood so effectively can rip flesh and bone with little trouble.

If you bought the tree for $6 and cut the trunk into three lengths, two 12-foot lengths and one 6-foot length, you will use 5 gallons of gas and two quarts of oil. You will end the job with 12 lengths of siding and three squared logs, with the combined worth of many times the cost of your investment.

The finished siding would cost about $12 if you bought it from a dealer. You can saw three or four, possibly more, lengths of siding in an hour, saving as close to $50 per hour by doing the work yourself.

Oak, pine, and a number of other trees can be used for siding. If you don't own your own source of trees, trees can still be found in a number of ways: farmers might want to clear new land for cultivation; when storms blow down many trees in either rural or urban areas; or when the federal government issues permits to cut in national forests or other protected areas. You can even buy trees from farmers or other landowners. If a timber cutter buys a tract of forest land, he will pay the owner about $6 each for enormous trees. This price has been rather stable for years and is not likely to fluctuate greatly during the coming years.

While timber companies buy and cut entire stands of trees, you can often find a landowner who will permit you to do selective cutting of trees and leave the basic forest protected. You can ask for cutting rights to thin the trees. Assure the landowner that he can pick out and mark the trees he wishes to have cut and removed.

Once you have found the trees you'll use and before you begin cutting trees down, you need to determine how long your siding will be. Once you know the size you'll need, you can cut the tree trunks into basic lengths. Remember, you'll need various lengths, so don't turn away from shorter trees. It is very difficult to handle entire logs. Instead, cut off the siding, which can be handled and hauled more easily. The rest of the log can be cut into firewood or sold to sawmills.

For best results, all siding should be the same width. Even if the trees are of different sizes, you can mill the siding to the same widths very easily. Start by rolling, prying, or otherwise elevating the trunk of the tree, one end at a time, until the trunk is completely off the ground. There should be a clearance of at least 6 inches under the tree. All rocks, roots, and other objects that could interfere with the cutting should be cleared away from the area. See FIG. 10-6.

When the trunk is in place, place small shims, wedges, or chocks under the trunk to keep it from rolling. Then use a chalk line to mark the cutline.

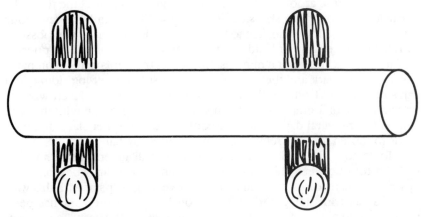

10-6 When cutting log siding, elevate the log so that it rests on two long logs or blocks so that the chain of the saw doesn't dig into the dirt and cause instant dulling.

All of your siding should be the same thickness, if possible. Use a rule to measure in 3 to 4 inches, whatever thickness you prefer, from the bark side of the tree trunk. Do this at both ends. Drive a small nail part way into the end of the tree trunk at the 3-inch or 4-inch point.

Loop the chalk line end over the first nail, lift the line high in order to get an accurate mark, and let the line fall over the end of the log. Carry the line to the other and wrap it around the other nail. Then snap the line. You might have to snap it two or three times to get a mark that is readily visible. See FIG. 10-7.

10-7 Use a chalk line to mark the cut line and then cut off the slab side of the log. Keep the chain saw in a vertical position to keep from getting an uneven cut.

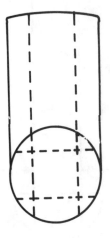

With your chain saw, cut a 2-inch groove along the chalk line along the entire length of the log. Stand on the opposite side of the log as you work so there is no danger that the saw can skip off the side of the log and gash your leg or foot.

When you have cut the groove, return to the starting point and ease the chain into the groove and cut nearly straight down until the tip of the bar reaches through the slab side of the trunk. Slowly pull the saw along the length of the log. Take care to hold the saw as straight as you possibly can. If the saw engine or head tilts to either side, the cut will be poor.

It will take you several minutes, but when the cut is made, you have, except for the bark and the trimming, your first length of log siding. You can strip the bark from the slab by using an axe, the blade of a crowbar or wrecking bar, or a similar tool. If you stack the siding length with the bark still on it for several days while you continue to cut other slabs, the bark tends to loosen for easy removal, in many cases, by hand.

To remove the bark while the siding is still green, insert any flat pointed tool between the cambium layer and the solid wood and pry upward. In many cases, you can easily remove long strips of bark this way.

You can trim siding with the bark on it or after the bark has been removed. Often, trimming makes it easier to remove the bark. To trim, lay the siding bark-down on two lengths of wood at least 6 inches thick. Use a rule to determine how wide you can make the siding. If you are cutting 8-inch siding, mark the 8-inch cutline at one end of the siding. Go to the other end of the siding and mark an 8-inch section there as well. Strike a chalk line from one mark to the mark at the other end. Do this on both sides of the length. See FIG. 10-8. Use the chain saw to trim along the chalked line. Start by cutting an inch-deep groove along each chalk line. Then return to the starting point and complete the cuts. You now have a finished length of siding.

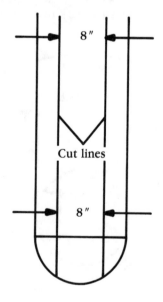

8"

Cut lines

8"

10-8   When the slab is cut away, lay the slab, cut side up, and mark the edge cuts.

The entire process for one length of siding will take 15 minutes or slightly longer, depending on the size of the tree and the length of the log, as well as upon your physical condition and skill with the saw.

When the first piece of siding is cut, roll the log until it rests on the cut surface. Mark and cut the second length of siding. You can go to the opposite side of the log and rip the third length. At this point, you can roll the log once again and rip the fourth length of siding.

When you are finished, you will have a nearly square log left. This log can be used for a solid log wall, if you wish to construct one, or, at worst, it can be cut into firewood lengths and split for fuel. A much better use is to use the same principles used earlier and cut the squared log into rough timbers. You can cut 2-×-6 timbers or virtually any dimension you want.

When you have finished with the cutting, stack the lengths of siding to air dry. Stack them in a square so that each length will be exposed to air on all surfaces. Let them dry for several weeks if possible.

When you install the siding onto the wall of the house, stagger the butt-joining locations. Do not let consecutive logs joint at the same point anywhere on the wall. You will also need to chink or seal between log units. Even a tiny space between the units will permit water and air to pass into the house.

LOG KITS

There are several companies that specialize in cutting and selling entire kits for log houses. Because the log house interior wall is also the exterior wall, there is a question of whether these walls are actually siding. Whatever the answer, you can create a beautiful log house with kits.

When you buy a kit, you will receive only the logs, in many, if not most, cases. You will not receive flooring, roofing, ceiling, molding, deck lumber, or any of the other necessities. You will generally receive only the logs for the walls. In some cases, the logs for interior walls might be included. Therefore, make certain you and the dealer agree on what you will receive when the shipment arrives before you buy. Determine how much help, if any, you will have in erecting the walls.

The kits usually contain beautiful logs with excellent workmanship. A spline system is included with many of the kits, and chinking is largely done when the kit is assembled. The costs of these kits vary anywhere from $15,000 to several times that amount, and the size of the finished house will vary similarly.

If you want to cut your own logs and build your house, you can do so with a great deal of hard work and painstaking effort. The effort is repaid by the house you get for your troubles.

You can cut your own logs for a house 32 feet wide and 52 feet long for about the same cost as 10 panels of exterior plywood. Seen from another perspective, covering a house the same size would require 42 panels of plywood, which would cost about eight times as much as the logs would cost if you cut them yourself.

Remember that with the solid logs, you get both interior and exterior walls, saving you the cost of all the framing and interior wall covering that would be required if you built a traditional frame house. You also save the money needed for insulation and sheathing. You can erect the walls of a log house, if you cut your own, for only a fraction of what traditional framing costs, and you will have a wall that is stronger, more durable, and far better insulated. See FIG. 10-9.

10-9 If you use the entire log, you can square the logs or use them rounded. Squared logs are easy to handle and can serve as both interior and exterior walls.

ERECTING A LOG WALL

A log wall is a simple structure. Lay the first log along the foundation wall and drive fluted spikes through the log and into the sills. You will need to drill holes for the spikes before you sink them. Lay out and spike one complete course of logs.

Use a butt-and-pass system for the logs. This means that, on the first course, the long side logs will extend one foot past the foundation wall and the short side logs will butt into the longer logs. On the second course, the short side logs will extend one foot past the long logs and the long side logs will butt into the shorter logs. See FIG. 10-10.

In every course, drill holes and spike the logs together. Countersink the spikes so that they firmly secure the two logs together. Sink a spike every two feet along each course.

You can frame window openings as soon as the top log is the height of the bottom of the window. You can build the rough window frame and install it, bracing it securely to keep it plumb. Then butt the ends of the

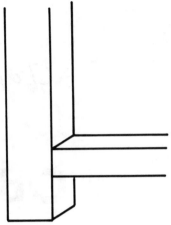

10-10 When you butt-join logs, spike through the long log and into the end of the shorter log. This type of corner is much easier than dove-tailed joining.

logs against the framing and drive 60d nails through the rough opening timbers and into the ends of the logs. Treat door frames the same way. Brace the rough framing until the logs are attached to it. Continue the butt-and-pass system until the wall has reached the desired height.

Cut your logs as long as you can manage. Join or splice logs only when necessary.

You'll find that the work is very tiring and, at times, it can be rather dangerous. You will assuredly need someone to help you, and if you can obtain the use of a forklift or similar lifting machinery, your work will be much easier.

Consult an experienced builder or refer to books on log houses before you invest a great deal of time and money. It is very possible that totally inexperienced persons can build their own log house from the ground up if they will only research the basics of log building. Log houses can be frustrating, but they are far more likely to be very rewarding, both from a financial and an aesthetic viewpoint.

Chapter **11**

Other sidings

*T*here are do-it-yourselfers who, for reasons of their own, do not want clapboard, vinyl, brick, concrete block, or combinations of these popular sidings. If you are among these, you have many other possibilities to choose from. Some of the other possibilities are aluminum, concrete, steel, and log siding. Some sources include glass as an alternative siding, but this might be stretching the concept more than a little. Siding is, by definition, building material such as boards, bricks, metals, or plastics that makes up the exposed surface of outside walls of frame buildings.

A solid brick wall, which has no framing as such, is not considered a wall with brick siding. If the house is framed and a brick veneer is then installed over the sheathing, then the bricks are considered siding materials.

It is possible to consider concrete blocks as a form of siding only if there is framing. In this book, concrete blocks are discussed only because interior walls are often installed to cover the interior framing, but this distinction is somewhat vague.

Glass walls, as such, do not have interior or exterior framing and glass is not properly considered a siding material. There are many houses with large glass plates, some of which cover the entire wall, but there is no inner material to be covered and, therefore, the glass is not siding in the strictest sense.

ALUMINUM

One of the early popular siding materials was aluminum, which has remained a staple building material over the years. Years ago, aluminum ranked behind forest products and bricks as the most popular siding in the nation. An estimated 10 percent of all houses were covered with aluminum siding. Today, aluminum accounts for about 3 percent of all siding surfaces. According to reports issued by construction marketers, wood, brick, vinyl, hardboard, and stucco rank ahead of aluminum.

The major advantages of aluminum are that it is lightweight, durable, relatively inexpensive, easy to install, and weather resistant. Aluminum is also low in maintenance cost. Finally, it can be used on either new buildings or over existing surfaces.

The surface of aluminum siding is baked on at the factory so that there is seldom a need to paint the surface. Usually, all that is required is an occasional washing with a garden hose, brushes, and ladder. The siding is manufactured to resemble painted wood.

Aluminum can be installed successfully over bricks, concrete blocks, wood, stucco, and several other conventional sidings. The major consideration is that the surface under the aluminum be in good shape. Wood that is rotted or termite-infested is not a proper substructure for siding of any type.

One attractive style of aluminum siding is the imitation clapboard style. The shadow effect created by the clapboard design causes the surface of the house to look like wood while still retaining its effective watershed ability.

While the most popular type of aluminum siding is the time-honored white board effect, aluminum siding is now available in a wide variety of colors and styles. One company offers nine distinct colors. Aluminum siding can be bought in widths of 4 inches, double or twin 4-inch style, 8-inch style, and up to 12 inches. The siding is also available in vertical as well as horizontal panels. You can choose a smooth or textured finish in the siding, and insulated siding that offers better protection against heating and cooling loss is also available. Chapter 6 details how to measure for the amount of siding you will need to do the job.

Installing aluminum siding

To install aluminum siding, you'll need the following tools or articles of equipment: saw (crosscut, circular, or hacksaw), tin snips, hammer, chalk line, measuring tape or rule, level, carpenter's square, caulk gun, aviation snips, and the proper nails. If you use a circular saw, be sure you have the proper blade for cutting aluminum.

One problem that worried many home owners was the danger of the metal siding in contact with the electrical wiring of the house. Modern builders as well as the Aluminum Siding Association strongly recommend that you connect a wire, no smaller than Number 8, to some point on the siding and then run the wire to either the electric ground near the meter base or to the cold water lines. Be sure to use Underwriters Laboratories-approved connectors.

Aluminum siding manufacturers include detailed instructions on how to install the siding. The panels themselves go up easily. The more difficult steps are installing aluminum around doors, windows, and soffits.

A frequent method of installation includes nailing up a starter strip at the wall line where the wall meets the foundation. Chapter 7 details how to strike a chalk line after using a line level or measuring tape to locate the proper low points and starting points on the wall. Once the starter strip is nailed in place (using the pre-punched holes) by nailing into the studs behind the rigid sheathing, the first panel clips onto the strip and the top of the panel is nailed to the studs. The second panel clips onto the previous panel and the top, again, is nailed to the stud. Pre-punched holes are provided for your convenience.

Before you nail in any permanent panels, strike the chalk line and, as a double measure, use a tape to measure from the soffit to the chalked line. The distance should be the same on both ends of the wall. You can also use a story pole, which is a long board with the points marked where the top of each panel should come.

It is a good idea to use both a measuring tape and the story pole. To make a story pole, use a 2×4. Stand the 2×4 beside the corner and mark the point where the chalked line crosses the 2×4. Next, determine how much weather surface there will be on each panel you install. If the "to-the-weather" surface is 8 inches, then mark the story pole at every 8-inch gradation. Then, when you begin to install the panels, you can hold the story pole up to the corner at each end of the wall and check to be certain that you are staying on course.

If you see a discrepancy, stop and make the necessary corrections at once. Don't try to absorb the discrepancy by adjusting subsequent panels. The panels must clip onto the previous panel precisely. No free play is allowed.

When you nail up the starter strips and panels, drive nails in until they are holding snugly but not too tight.

Before panels are installed, nail the corner posts in place. The bottom of the corner posts should line up exactly with the chalked line made earlier. The corner posts have channels on each side, and later, the ends of the siding panels will fit into these channels for a weatherproof joint.

Door and window trim

The next step is to install the door and window trim. Use the same procedure as with vinyl panels that was covered in chapters 6 and 7. When you are ready for the panels, start by hooking the first panel onto the starter strip and then nailing the panel to the studs. Continue progressing all the way up the wall.

When you must lap the siding, arrange it so that the lap is away from the most frequent traffic. As you face the doorway, lap it so that the panel nearest you is on top of the panel that meets it from the other end. This way, when you look down the wall, the lap is not as noticeable as it would be if the lap were toward you.

When you cut the siding panels to fit in the spaces between doors and windows, remember to allow a 1/4-inch space for expansion and contraction. If necessary, trim the last course so that it will fit under the eaves.

Nail in the underseal strips to seal the wall against moisture. Link the top of the panel to the undersill and lock it into place.

STUCCO

Another way of adding siding to your house is to apply a stucco exterior. This type of siding or exterior wall covering can add a great deal of attractiveness at low cost. Better yet, you don't need sophisticated equipment with which to do the job.

You can choose from a host of natural color or artificial hues. Cement itself is either a light tan or beige color or part of the gray family. You can also paint the finished stucco exterior to your own preference.

There are two popular ways to apply stucco. It can be applied over lath strips of galvanized or zinc-coated metal and attached to the existing wall. The stucco is then spread over the metal. The metal, which has fairly large holes in it, allows the stucco to penetrate through the holes, and when the stucco sets or hardens, the material that penetrated through the holes holds the entire coating securely in place.

You can also buy woven wire screens that can be attached to the walls. The stucco permeates the screen or woven fabric and holds the coating in place. There is also a 2-×-2-inch mesh wire fabric with a paper backing or a 1-inch mesh with no backing. The mesh is installed over furring or a similar material to keep the mesh at least 1/4 inch from the sheathing. The space between the mesh and the sheathing forces the stucco through to provide maximum holding power.

The second way to install stucco is to make a stucco mortar and spread it like plaster—except that it has no lath—over the wall. If you choose to install stucco without lath, mix a one-to-three mixture of one part Portland cement to three parts sand, mixed into a plastic texture with water. Don't try to spread mortar that is too dry or too thin. If the mortar is too dry, it will crumble and fall from the wall. If it is too thin, it will run off the wall almost as soon as it is applied.

Spread the stucco thinly over concrete blocks in three or four coatings. Let the first coating dry thoroughly and then add a second coating. Each coat should be about 1/4 inch thick. The final coat should result in a final thickness of about 1 inch of stucco.

If you plan to add stucco over any type of surface except concrete block, start with plywood sheathing. Cover the plywood sheathing with building paper and then cover it with the lath materials. The stucco is then spread over the lath. Do not apply stucco over sheathing or plywood. Some form of lath must be used to keep the stucco from making direct contact with the wood or sheathing.

STEEL

In recent years, steel has become a readily available building material and comes in panels that are flat, striated, or in a variety of other designs.

Some panels are steel only, but others are polyurethane-insulated for better protection against heating and cooling loss. Some of the steel panels are covered with exterior aggregate stone. These panels are very strong as well as durable. The panels do not carry weight as load-bearing walls do, although some are capable of load-bearing. Consult dealers for specific details in this regard or ask your local building inspector about restrictions.

Steel panels are available in a wide range of colors, including trims with contrasting colors. You can buy kits especially suited for room additions or for buildings 30×40 feet with 10-foot ceilings. These kits include steel panels with the framing and even the roof.

Steel panels are installed in several ways. Some use self-tapping screws. Others have concealed fasteners. Still others are bolted together. Because of the weight of these panels, you'll need a second person to help you lift the panels into place and hold them while you secure them.

There are a number of other siding materials that can be used, and one of the most interesting is log siding, or whole logs, which are used as interior and exterior walls. Chapter 9 covers logs and log sidings in detail.

CONCRETE SIDING

One of the newer siding products available today is a non-asbestos concrete that comes in sections or boards. These products are reputed to be as hard as concrete but not nearly as heavy. The units are classified as fiber concrete and are guaranteed to last for 50 years and to resist saltwater and other enemies of house siding. The materials are also highly resistant to impact and corrosion. They are also fire-resistant. Finally, they have the advantage of being extremely strong and durable, yet flexible.

Concrete sections, or boards, are installed the same as other siding—over the sheathing and wall framing. See FIG. 11-1. Some of the units can be bought in 9-inch-wide sections, 12 feet long, 3/8 inch thick, and with up to 2 inches of lap. The weight is considerable, but usually two men can manage it. See FIG. 11-2.

The concrete siding can be painted or it can be given a wood grain effect. To cut the units, use a carbide-tipped blade or diamond blade. You can also score and break units (see FIG. 11-3). Figure 11-4 is a look at the installed product.

These concrete planks create a visual effect that is as attractive as siding and durable as concrete—up to 50 years. See FIGS. 11-5 and 11-6. You can buy concrete panels that produce an equally attractive siding. See FIG. 11-7.

If you have any concrete planks left over, consider them to enhance the overall landscape and tie in with the house design. They can be used effectively in privacy walls and other decorative features. See FIG. 11-8 for a sample of how a concrete plank fence looks.

Use galvanized, hot-dip, 6-box siding nails. Nails should penetrate at least 1 1/2 inches into the studding. Do not drive in nails near the edge of the units to prevent cracking. If you still notice a tendency toward cracking, pre-drill holes in the concrete and then nail as you ordinarily would.

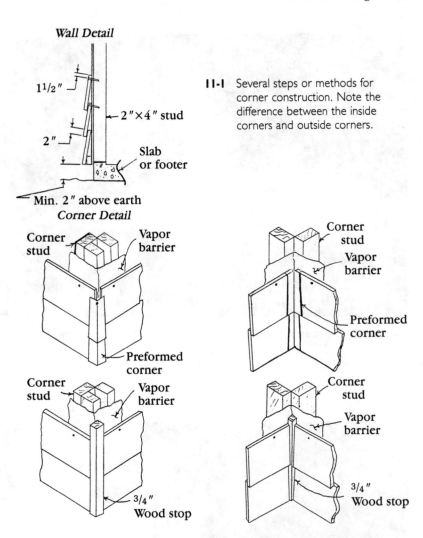

Wall Detail

$1\frac{1}{2}$"

2"×4" stud

2"

Slab or footer

Min. 2" above earth

Corner Detail

Corner stud

Vapor barrier

Preformed corner

Corner stud

Vapor barrier

3/4" Wood stop

Corner stud

Vapor barrier

Preformed corner

Corner stud

Vapor barrier

3/4" Wood stop

11-1 Several steps or methods for corner construction. Note the difference between the inside corners and outside corners.

11-2 You will need help if you are installing concrete planks. The weight is too much for one person to lift, hold, and nail.

11-3   Proper methods and equipment for cutting concrete planks and panels.

11-4   Panels after installation.

11-5 and 11-6 Concrete planks look like traditional siding but have the strength and durability of concrete.

11-7 Concrete panels create attractive sidings. Note the use of trim work with the panels.

11-8 Any leftover units can be used for outbuilding purposes or for privacy fences.

You can also use self-tapping screws sunk into metal studs if you wish. Pre-drilling will be necessary. When installing these units, a better appearance often results if you stagger the panels on the wall face rather than have all of the joints occur at the same level.

You can use H-profile joiners when you are joining units or you can butt the ends of the panels together. Caulk anywhere the joints are made by butting, and all butt joints should be made over a stud.

These concrete panels can be used in commercial, industrial, or residential buildings. The products in this line of building materials can also be used for fascias, soffits, gables, and various accent areas.

Chapter 12

Siding accessories

*A*fter the siding is installed, you might want to add several items that will help define the character of your house. This might include shutters, guttering, and lattice, among other additions.

SHUTTERS

On most houses, an attractive system of shutters can add greatly to the overall beauty and impressiveness of the house. These shutters can be installed with little effort and at a very reasonable cost.

Decades ago, shutters were utilitarian. They were added to the house for no other reasons than for protection against storms, loss of heat, and intruders. Today, because many houses have storm windows and other protective elements, shutters are for cosmetic purposes only.

One of the major reasons for including shutters many years ago is that the shutters protected the window glass, which, at that time, was not only rather scarce but extremely rare. Today's shutters are intended to decorate and to provide visual appreciation of the house. They can be installed beside windows and doors. See FIGS. 12-1 and 12-2.

Well-chosen shutters can provide the visual illusion of widening the window, making it appear larger and more elegant. Shutters also help to stress the lines of a house, adding variety to an otherwise unbroken expanse of bricks, vinyl, wood boards, or other siding materials.

Older shutters were hinged so that the two panels could be pulled closed and fastened. Modern shutters contain no hinges; the shutters themselves do not move. They are fastened to the wall on both sides so that movement, even if desired, is impossible.

When you are planning your house, plan your shutters along with the remainder of the building. Choose standard-sized windows for a variety of reasons, one of which is so that you can have standard shutters

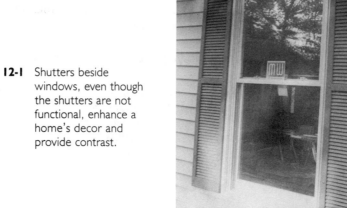

12-1 Shutters beside
windows, even though
the shutters are not
functional, enhance a
home's decor and
provide contrast.

12-2 A modest house lacking distinctive qualities can be greatly improved by adding
shutters.

readily available. If you find that you must special-order shutters, you will also find that the cost rises greatly.

Shutter height is in accordance with the height of the most frequently purchased windows. The width of shutters can vary from 14 to 20 inches, with intermediate widths of 16 and 18 inches. See TABLE 12-1 for a list of shutter heights and window openings.

Table 12-1 Window Sizes

Shutter Height (inches)	Fits Window Opening (inches)	Approx. Weight Per Pair (pounds)
25	22–26	5
35	32–36	6
39	36–40	7
43	40–44	8
47	44–48	$8^{1}/_{2}$
51	48–52	9
55	52–56	$9^{1}/_{2}$
59	56–60	10
63	60–64	$10^{1}/_{2}$
67	64–68	$11^{1}/_{2}$
71	68–72	12
81	76–82	13

Keep the width in mind as you are planning your house. If your power base is too near a window, there will not be room for a shutter on that side. Guttering, lattice work, and even doors placed too near windows can prevent shutter installation.

You can purchase shutters made from wood, vinyl, aluminum, or nylon. These units are lightweight and easily handled by one person. You can, if you wish, find shutters that are hinged so that they can be used rather than admired.

Installing shutters

If you want to use your shutters for privacy and protection, you can hinge them to the window trim so that they will close and lock and cover the window completely. If you want decoration only, you can attach the shutters in place by using screws, screws in anchors, or nails. Of the three most frequent types of installation, the screws in anchors are perhaps the most satisfactory. Work moves better and faster if you have a helper.

One of the accepted methods of installing shutters requires an electrical drill, a small bit and a larger bit, and the anchors, which are plastic devices that can be slipped into a pre-drilled hole in the mortar or wood of the siding adjacent to the window. The size of the bits depends on the size of the anchors and the screws to be used. When you buy the screws, ask the dealer to provide the appropriate anchors and bits as well.

The bit for the anchors should be large enough to allow the anchor to be tapped into position comfortably. If the hole is too tight and you must drive the anchor in place, the anchor will split and break and the screw will not go into position readily.

When you start, have a helper hold the shutter in place while you drill the first holes, the ones for the screws. With the shutter in the actual position where it will be installed, you can see the mortar joint or other surface where the anchor must be installed. Avoid nail heads or other obstacles.

Use the smaller bit, the one that is the size of the shank of the screw, first. Drill two holes at the top and two at the bottom of the shutter. Let the bit go through the framing of the shutter and contact with the surface under the shutter. Do not try to drill through the mortar with the drill bit used on the shutter frame. You will dull the bit and not be able to use it for the rest of the work.

When you have drilled all four holes, one in each corner of the framing and at least an inch from any edge, take the shutter down and then use the masonry bit (if you are installing shutters over a brick surface or concrete block surface) and drill holes for the anchors. The holes need be only deep enough to allow the anchors to be seated flush with the surface of the bricks or mortar.

You can see the marks made by the first drill bit. To drill into mortar or other masonry surface, position the point of the drill exactly where you want it, hold the drill perfectly parallel with the ground, or horizontally, and apply moderate pressure. Do not let the bit jump and skip around. Press the trigger to the drill all the way down and run the drill at full speed. Eye and hand protection are desirable for this work.

When you have drilled the four holes, insert the screws into the holes drilled into the shutter framing and then hold the shutter back into place. Use a power screwdriver or manual screwdriver to drive the screws into the anchors. Tighten the screws snugly. Do not overtighten; you might scratch or scar the shutter itself.

The principle behind the anchor is simple. The plastic anchor fits snugly into the predrilled hole. When you drive in the screw, the shank of the screw forces the anchor to widen and, thus, tighten against the walls of the hole. When the screw is fully driven, it and the anchor will hold firmly against great pressure. The shutter will not work loose in wind or other ordinary pressure and your work will last for decades under normal circumstances.

If you do not want the expense of buying a power screwdriver or the slowness of using a manual screwdriver, you can buy a small attachment for your drill. These attachments cost only a few cents and come in a variety of slot-head and Phillips-head types. You can buy a small packet of assorted attachments for a dollar or two.

To use the attachments, simply use the chuck key for your drill to open the chuck and remove the drill bit. Then slip the attachment into the chuck and tighten. Most drills have a forward and reverse direction and you can install screws or remove them simply by moving a switch from one position to another.

You can save time and effort by holding and marking all shutters you plan to install. Do the same with shutter panels for your doors, if you plan to install them. When all the drilling is done and the anchor points are marked, you are finished with the smaller bit.

Next, drill the holes for all of the anchors. Then change the drill to install the screwdriver attachment and install all of the shutters. By doing the work this way, you won't have to stop to change drill bits. The obvious exception is if you are working from a scaffold, it is much easier to change bits than it is to move the scaffold. By all means, do all the work necessary on that scaffold before moving it.

It is even better to have several drills, if you can borrow extras. One drill can hold the smaller bit, the other can have the masonry bit, and the third will hold the screwdriver attachment. Even if this is unrealistic, changing bits does not require a great deal of time.

GUTTERS

Gutters serve one purpose: they collect rainwater or other moisture that runs from the roof of the house and transport the water away from the house's foundation. This is important because water seeping around the foundation can lead to damp or wet basements, mildew, and decay, as well as insect infestation.

Gutters, sometimes called eaves troughs, take the water to downspouts, located generally at the corners of the house, and from there, the water is diverted away from the house. You can also buy and install plastic pipes to connect to downspouts to take the water a considerable distance from the house.

Guttering comes in several surfaces. You can buy guttering that is prepainted so that it will never need painting. Some of the vinyl products never need any type of maintenance, and aluminum is essentially the same. You can install wood gutters or you can buy guttering made from aluminum, vinyl, or other materials.

Wood gutters are made from redwood or other treated wood and are frequently shaped like a squared U. The joints where the three main pieces of wood are connected are always sealed to prevent leakage. The end of the trough is closed off with a wood block, and the joints are again sealed. You can construct these gutters on the ground and then lift them into position and attach them to the fascia or to the ends of rafters if you do not plan to add a fascia. Most people prefer to buy their guttering rather than to make it, although wood gutters, if properly cared for, can last generally as long as the house stands.

The one great problem is that of standing water. Be sure to have the gutters slope downward slightly from the middle of the house so that all collected water will be diverted to the downspouts and away from the house.

Installing guttering

Metal or vinyl gutters are far more popular than are wood gutters. When you buy guttering, you will also buy the joint connectors, corners (if any are needed), end blocks, brackets, and nails. To install guttering, you'll need a hammer, drill and long bit, nails, hacksaw, and pliers or a screwdriver. Figure 12-3 shows the materials you'll need and the steps to follow when installing guttering.

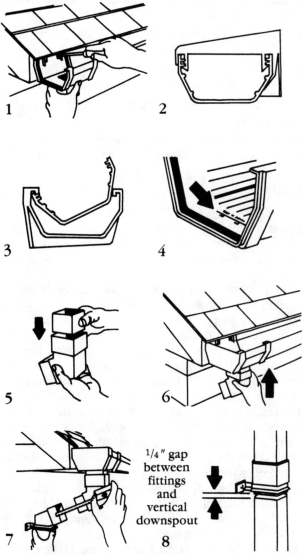

12-3 Components of a guttering system and how they are installed, step-by-step. Leave a ¼-inch gap between fittings and the vertical downspout(s).

The guttering will consist, when all the work is done, of the gutter itself, slip joint connectors, end caps, end pieces, downspout, elbows, pipe straps, hangers, spikes and ferrules, and a pipe strainer (if used):

- Slip joint connectors are metal slots that allow one length of guttering to fit into another.
- End caps fit against the end of the guttering to keep water from running out of the ends rather than down the downspout.
- End pieces are short sections of guttering that contain an opening for the downspout.
- Elbows are angled lengths of guttering that permit you to turn corners.
- Pipe straps wrap around the downspout and allow you to fasten the downspout to the wall.
- Hangers are thin strips that wrap completely around the guttering to hold it together.
- Pipe strainer fits over the top opening of the downspout to filter out objects that will clog or close the downspout.
- A spike is used to hold the guttering in place.
- A ferrule is a thin collar or sheathe, usually metal, through which a spike or shaft can be inserted.

Once your scaffolding, if needed, is in place, you can begin to install the guttering in a variety of ways. One simple way is to start by using a line level and chalk line to determine the amount of fall, or downward slope, needed.

Have a helper hold the line level at one end of the roofline (or you can drive a nail partway in and hook the level line over the nail) and take the other end to the opposite corner. When you have found the perfect level, mark both ends of the line. Then use a chalk line to strike a line all the way across the roofline. You might need to strike the line in several segments if your line is not long enough. It is very important that the line be perfectly level. Your entire slope system depends on this first line.

After the line is made, determine how much fall you want or need. This fall is stated in terms of inches of slope in relation to running feet in length. A fall of 1 inch per 10 feet will equal 4 inches over a 40-foot distance. You can see that such a fall is unrealistic, but if the house is 40 feet long and you slope the guttering in both directions, the fall is only 2 inches for 20 feet, which is much better.

The fall is still too great, however, because the disparity between the guttering and the fascia will be unattractive. You will like the result better if you use a fall of 1 inch for 12 feet, if the roofline is relatively short, or 1 inch for 16 feet if the roofline is longer.

For a roofline of 40 feet, use a 1 to 12 slope. If the roofline is 50 feet or longer, use a slope of 1 inch to 16 feet. You might have to decrease the slope even more if the results are unsatisfactory. Just don't decrease the slope until the water will not flow readily.

After the line is chalked, find and mark the midpoint of the roofline. Once you have determined the amount of fall or slope you need, strike another line to guide the slope calculation (see FIG. 12-4).

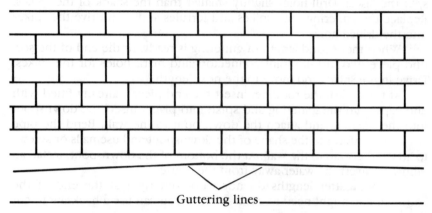

Guttering lines

12-4   To ensure that your guttering has the right fall, chalk a level line from the middle of the fascia board to the end of the wall. Determine the drop and measure down an inch or two and chalk a second line.

Assume that the house is 44 feet long. The midpoint is then at the 22-foot mark. If you want to have a total slope or fall of 1¹/₂ inches from the midpoint, go to the corner of the house and measure down 1¹/₂ inches from the first line. Then strike a chalk line from the lower mark to the midpoint so that the new line joins the first line at the middle of the roofline.

When you are ready to install the guttering, let the top of the guttering follow the second, or slanted, line you made. The first line should be very close to the roof sheathing at the top of the fascia boards. The slanted line should end near a point halfway down the fascia board's width.

Drill holes in the guttering so that you can install the spikes and ferrules. The spikes must go all the way through the guttering trough and into the wood of the fascia. The ferrules slip over the spikes inside the guttering and keep the guttering from collapsing or folding inward. See FIG. 12-5.

12-5   When installing spikes and ferrules, start the spike through the outside hole and slip the ferrule over the end of the spike. Slide the spike through the ferrule and out the back hole. Finally, drive the spike into the fascia board or rafter ends, depending on how the guttering will be attached.

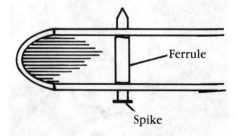

Ferrule

Spike

Drill the holes in the guttering and then hold the gutter in place so you can mark the spots where you will need to drill into the wood in order to sink the spikes. If you do not predrill, the spikes might bend or split the fascia. Drill holes slightly smaller than the shank of the spikes. Replace the guttering with spikes and ferrules and then drive the spikes into the drilled holes.

When the second length of guttering is ready, fit the end of the second piece into the slip joint connectors and mark holes for the spikes. Drive in the spikes and move to the next length.

At the end of the roofline, insert the end pieces, already fitted with end caps, into the guttering and spike into place. Insert the downspout into the opening and attach the downspout to the wall. Bend the pipe straps to conform to the shape of the downspout and use nails or screws to attach the strap to the wall. At the bottom of the downspout, install an elbow to divert the water away from the house.

If your gutter lengths do not work out right at the end of the roofline, you might need to cut a section. You can use a hacksaw to cut the sections.

When you are installing the guttering, keep a level handy and use it to see that you do not accidentally let the section slip and spoil the slope or fall. Double-check before any spikes are installed. When the installation is complete, go back and caulk the joints to prevent leakage.

LATTICE

Lattice is a crisscross type of wood strips, vinyl, or other materials that can be installed in sections. Lattice permits free circulation of air as well as admitting light. At the same time, lattice can provide privacy and a degree of security. See FIG. 12-6.

12-6 Lattice dresses up the space under a porch or deck and provides privacy and a measure of protection from stray animals.

Lattice is often installed under decks, around porches, or around gardens or outdoor sitting areas. The sections are very lightweight and installation is easy. Lattice under decks or porches can add greatly to the beauty and to the enjoyment of that area of the house.

Along the end or side of the house, you can install lattice enclosures for privacy enclosures so that the entrance of the house is concealed from public view. See FIGS. 12-7 and 12-8. Many people like to enclose garbage cans, clotheslines, sitting areas, backyard patios, and other spaces with lattice structures.

12-7 Otherwise-plain entrances can be enhanced with lattice.

For vegetable or flower gardens you can use lattice for low fences and attractive entrances or gateways. Such additions can protect the vegetation while increasing the aesthetic appeal of the area. See FIG. 12-9.

You can use wood lattice or some of the artificial materials such as vinyl. Vinyl will not decay and is not subject to insect attack. It never needs painting and will not warp.

You can buy narrow strips of wood and make your own lattice or you can buy the sections—wood or vinyl. If you make your own, you will need to buy wood strips that are about 2 inches wide and of whatever thickness you want. Half inch thickness is acceptable.

12-8 Lattice around storage and utility areas provides privacy as well as enhancing aesthetics.

12-9 Lattice gates and gardens or patio entrances can add greatly to the beauty of a house and outdoor areas.

Installing lattice

You will need to determine the size of the openings you want and lay out the sections. Nail the cross strips diagonally to the top and bottom rails and later to the end rails. Use small nails and cut the strips with a handsaw or with a fine-toothed circular saw blade.

If you buy lattice, position the sections where you want them and begin fastening at the top and middle. If you start at the ends or at the sides, the sections will tend to sag, resulting in a crooked installation.

You can fasten with nails, screws, or with staples. Some commercially prepared lattice sections need bracing. Follow installation instructions for the particular type of material you choose.

PORCH RAILINGS

If you have a porch or deck, you will find that adding railing to the deck, particularly if it is high, will be a requirement to meet the building code regulations. Such railing greatly enhances the deck, even if it is low, and adds greatly to the overall beauty of the siding for your house. See FIGS. 12-10 and 12-11.

12-10 Porch rails add beauty and balance.

12-11 Low porches can be improved by adding a wall or railing.

You can buy manufactured railing sections or you can build your own. Do-it-yourself railings are far more economical and, in many cases, stronger and more durable, depending upon the materials you use.

Railings, if you choose to build them, should be at least 3 feet high. If your house is long, higher railings, up to 40 inches, will look better. See FIG. 12-12.

12-12 This railing is 56-feet long and about 4-feet high. The added height is needed to achieve the desired effect for the extra length of the porch.

An easy and attractive way to build railing is to start with posts positioned 5 or so feet apart. To make these posts, use treated 2×4s. Cut one length 40 inches long and the other longer so that it will reach to the bottom of the porch or deck sills. The added length might be 8 to 10 inches. See FIG. 12-13.

Installing porch railings

If necessary, cut back the porch or deck overhang so that the longer length can be fitted against the sill and still remain in a vertical position. Connect the two lengths by using nails, bolts, or screws. The tops should be even. Bolts work best, because there is no danger that they will pull free. See FIG. 12-14.

Position the post so that the longer one rests against the sill. Using a long drill bit, drill two holes about 4 inches apart through the 2×4 and through the sill. Then insert long bolts and fasten the post to the deck.

Do this at every 5-foot point. If your deck or porch is an unusual length, spacing might be slightly different. Space posts so they retain a

12-13 Use doubled 2-×-4 timbers for rail posts, spaced about 5 feet apart. The back 2 × 4 actually extends past the deck flooring where it is bolted to the deck joists, as shown in FIG. 12-14.

12-14 The longer 2 × 4 is lower than the deck and is bolted to the deck framing. The shorter 2 × 4 ends flush with the deck floor.

symmetrical look. Do not have distances varying greatly between the posts. For extra safety and for added stability, you can use dowels and glue as well as bolts.

If you want to use dowels, buy dowel lengths and cut them into 3-inch lengths. Drill a hole into the bottom of the posts and another hole into the flooring. Coat the dowel with glue, on both ends, and insert one end of the dowel into the post and then insert the other end into the hole in the flooring. Then drill holes and install bolts. See FIG. 12-15.

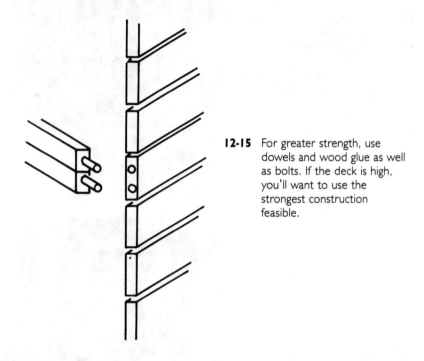

12-15 For greater strength, use dowels and wood glue as well as bolts. If the deck is high, you'll want to use the strongest construction feasible.

When all posts are installed, assemble your railing sections. A good plan is to leave a space below the bottom rail that is equal to the width of the 2×4s you are using. The bottom rail should be exactly long enough to reach from one post to the next. The top rail should reach halfway across each of the posts. If you have long timbers, you can allow them to cross several posts. The length is not crucial as long as the top rail ends halfway across the posts, except the first and last one. In these cases, the rail should reach across the entire post.

When the top rail is installed, decide on the best spacing for the balusters. If there is 5 feet between posts, there is a total of 60 inches. Divide the distance in terms of distance between balusters and the thickness of the balusters. The 2×4 will be 1½ inches thick.

If you leave 3 inches between baluster and post and between balusters, each baluster will need, including its own width, 4½ inches. If you leave 4 inches, each baluster, including its own thickness, will need 5½ inches. In other words, you can divide the space, then take half of that distance, then half of the remaining distance until you know exactly how wide apart your balusters must be and how many will be needed.

For a 5-foot length of railing, if you use 3¾-inch spacing, your first four balusters will need 15 inches. For a 60-inch space, you will need 16 balusters. The spacing includes the thickness of the baluster, so if you deduct the $1^1/2$-inch thickness, you will have a $2^1/4$-inch space between balusters.

You can create your own spacing arrangement to suit your own taste and to create the most economical arrangement. Once you have decided (as long as the spacing isn't wide enough to permit a child to fall through or get his head stuck), you can cut the lower rail and mark the baluster locations on it. Hold the bottom rail so that you can stand the end balusters under it and nail them through the bottom of the rail so that they are held securely.

Continue to nail all of the balusters in place. When you are done, place two short lengths of 2×4 against each post and turn the bottom rail to the bottom and rest the ends on the short lengths you have positioned. Then, use a level to get a vertical position for the balusters and nail through the top of the rail and into the ends of the balusters. Use galvanized nails to prevent rusting.

When this is done, toenail the bottom rail to the posts and then remove the 2-$\times$-4 lengths used for spacing. If you want your balusters $3^1/2$ inches apart, use a short length of 2×4 as a spacer.

It is much easier to fasten the bottoms if you can drive through the bottom rail. If you try to toenail the baluster in place after the rails are installed, there is very little room to hammer unless you toenail from the outside and, in this case, you will have trouble holding the baluster in place while you nail.

Chapter **13**

Finishing up

*A*s noted earlier, one of the major reasons for installing several types of siding is that maintenance is reduced to nearly a zero-level. Vinyl and other types of siding do not need to be painted—ever.

There are also a number of sidings that will need to be painted or stained, and nearly all types of siding should be nailed and caulked before the job is completely finished. This chapter deals with using the proper fasteners for the job, caulking and sealing joints, and applying paints and stains.

Once siding is installed, you need to make a thorough visual inspection to see that all nails are properly seated and that there are no loose ends of the job remaining. Before you begin to seal or paint, you should also clean the surfaces of all the installed materials thoroughly. Brush or sweep the panels or boards to remove clinging dust, sawdust, smears, and chalk lines. If necessary, use warm water, a sturdy cloth, and a detergent to remove stubborn stains and smears.

Observe all pertinent safety precautions before you begin work. Remove unused lumber, buckets, cartons, and remnants of siding materials. Be certain that the area where you intend to set up a ladder, if one is needed, is cleared so that the ladder can stand securely on level ground.

USING THE RIGHT FASTENERS

Some siding manufacturers will not guarantee their product unless the proper nails are used. In some wood, acid might cause many types of nails to deteriorate.

Many manufacturers recommend that stainless steel nails be used on several types of siding. Consult your dealer or read the manufacturer's installation directions carefully. Write or call the manufacturer if you cannot determine what nails should be used.

Stainless steel nails will cost more than other nails, but the extra cost is well repaid if the guarantee is to be honored if problems occur. The extra cost is minimal in most cases because so few nails are used in the installation of vinyl and aluminum siding.

Stainless steel nails

Corrosion-resistant nails are of primary importance for lumber and plywood construction materials, which are exposed to weather, high moisture, and other caustic conditions. Both the appearance and the structural performance of wood buildings are subject to rapid deterioration if fasteners corrode quickly. Because the cost of lumber is high and even modest building projects are fairly expensive, the added cost of stainless steel nails is not a financial burden, particularly if you consider the damage that might occur if galvanized nails are used.

According to published reports, if wood is chemically pressure-treated, corrosion is more serious. Laboratory tests have shown that stainless steel nails tend to corrode less than ordinary nails and the weight loss of the nails, as a result of corrosion and deterioration, is smaller than in ordinary nails. Even hot-dipped nails might suffer significantly when an acid reaction occurs. Moisture also contributes greatly to the destruction of many types of nails.

Wood siding nails

In modern building, nails are specifically engineered and manufactured for use with many wood siding materials. High-tensile stainless steel nails are said to be able to last the lifetime of whatever siding is used. Slender gauge and blunt points tend to minimize splitting and the generous underhead fillet permits the nail to be driven flush with the material surface without the expected cracking or crushing of the surrounding wood.

Many nails are manufactured with annular ring threads, whose strength is comparable to that of wood screws of similar length and gauge. Modern nails can be used below grade in wood construction of foundation walls.

Wood screws

Modern wood screws might be needed on some types of siding installation. Such screws are recommended for joints that will be exposed to the weather. New designs include self-countersinking heads; square-drive recess, deep enough to prevent driver bit cam-out; sharper points for faster penetration; self-tapping coarse threads requiring less driving force; and clear and nonstick coatings that lubricate for easier driving.

For finishing work, stainless steel screws small enough to be unobtrusive can also provide the strength and holding power needed. Such screws are good for use on fascia, soffit, corner boards, and mitered ends of siding.

DRIVING TIPS

Any carpenter or do-it-yourselfer will bend nails, but you can minimize bending nails and the danger to yourself and others if you will follow a few simple tips. First, the danger involved. In addition to that of damaged fingers, nails that have not penetrated deeply enough can fly through the air with considerable speed and force when they are hit. It is not uncommon for a nail to fly 15 to 20 feet, and the speed is great enough to damage eyes and exposed skin.

When you drive a nail, notice what the holding angle should be and drive the nail accordingly. If a board or other unit is to be nailed as close to another as possible, angle the nails slightly so that the point is angled toward the previous board. When you seat the nail, the final force of the hammer blows will drive the board in tightly against the other. If the nail is driven in straight or if it is angled the other way, the force of the blows is directed away from the adjacent board.

While you are hammering, look at the head of the nail rather than at the hammer. Grip the hammer near the end of the handle. If you grip the handle close to the hammer head, you tend to have less control of the tool and less force behind blows.

If you are nailing into wood that is well-cured and straight-grained, there is a tendency for the wood to split, particularly if the wood is old. To prevent splitting, try predrilling holes before nailing. The drill bit should be slightly smaller than the shank of the nail. Blunting the point of the nail can also help to reduce splitting. It might sound strange, but a blunt point will tear its way through the wood while a sharp point will penetrate too rapidly and split the wood. A blunted spike will not split wood that a sharp-pointed spike would damage.

Do not blunt the point severely. If you are working near a metal surface, hold the nail so that the point is against the surface and tap the head lightly a time or two.

When you are driving two nails into the end of the same board, angle the nail on the left so that the point is slightly toward the other nail. Angle the other nail so that the point is slightly toward the first nail. Imagine that the two nails are several inches longer. They should be angled so that the two shanks would cross each other.

If you are driving nails in an awkward position and you tend to hit your fingers as you start nails, hold the nail with a pair of pliers until it is fully started. Use a punch to seat nails that are used in surfaces that must be protected. If you hold the punch steadily and hit the punch, you will not mar the surface of the wood.

When you have to pull nails from wood, use a crowbar or similar tool rather than the claws of the hammer. If no other tools are handy, use the hammer claws but place a small flat length of wood under the hammer so you do not scratch the surface of the wood being installed. The elevated surface of the hammer head will also increase the leverage of the hammer.

If you are extracting nails from a very hard surface, there is a danger that the nail might suddenly spring free and become airborne. A shooting nail can also spring up and strike you in the face. To prevent this, place your free hand so that it cups the hammer claws and the nail. When the nail springs free it will be stopped painlessly by the palm of your hand.

If you are driving long screws into hard wood, drill a pilot hole before starting the screw. This hole can be slightly smaller than the shank of the screw but the hole itself will allow the screw to penetrate the wood much more easily without reducing the holding power of the screw.

You might find that dipping the screw into oil helps to seat the screw. If the screw shank is dry and perhaps rusty, the shank will not turn readily in hard wood. A small amount of lubrication can help turn the screw and seat more easily.

PAINTING AND STAINING

Many years ago, paints tended to be somewhat similar. Today, however, there is an amazing variety of paints. Some paints have an oil base while others have a latex base. Some paints dry within minutes while others need several hours. Some paints, usually oil-based paints, are very irritating to the noses, eyes, and throats of some people. If you tend to be bothered by the smell of paint, you might need to use a latex product.

Cleanup is also an important matter. Fresh latex paints can be cleaned with only warm water while oil-based paints require mineral spirits or paint thinner. Brushes used in latex paints can be cleaned in water, while brushes used in oil-based paints must be cleaned in a solvent.

The price of paint is also a matter of concern. Some paints are advertised at very low prices, but when you use the paints, you find that two or even three coats are needed for full coverage. A more expensive paint might have covered the surface well with one coat. Unless you know the product is a good one, you are engaging in false economy if you buy cheaper paints. If you have to paint the surface two or more times, you will probably pay more for the extra paint than you would have paid for high-quality paint in the first place. You should also consider that your time and energy needed for the extra coats is costly, too.

The short drying time of latex paints is not merely a convenience. In many ways, rapid drying helps you to get a better job for your time, money, and effort. Oil-based paints that take many hours to dry will tend to catch and hold undesirable elements. Sudden gusts of wind can blow dirt, leaf fragments, and other debris against the painted surface where they will stick. Bugs that fly into the wet paint can become stuck there, permanently.

Another advantage of latex paints is that latex paints are porous and, thus, allow moisture to escape from under the paint. Trapped moisture can cause damage through decay and insect attraction.

There are several instruments you can use to apply paint rather than the simple paintbrush of yesteryear. You can use a brush, foam pad, roller, or sprayer, to mention only a few of the applicators. If you use a brush, you will probably need to buy at least two brushes: one wide and one narrow. The wide brush is for broad, flat surfaces; the narrow is for trim work where neatness counts.

You can cover a great deal of space in a short time with a roller. The major disadvantages of rollers are that they tend to use a very large amount of paint and they are rather untidy to use. Dripping is a frequent problem, and even if you are outdoors, you must be concerned about dripping. Paint can stain foundation walls, shrubs, or flowers, but even if there is no danger of any problem in these areas, you are still wasting expensive paint.

The central question revolves around whether the time you save by using the roller is balanced by the extra money and the time needed for clean-up work. Often, the time saved is of great importance, and rollers are very effective when you are covering large expanses of easily painted surfaces.

The size of your paint tray, if you use a roller, is worth some consideration. Larger trays obviously hold more paint and need to be filled less frequently. This can be an advantage if you are working in a hard-to-reach area where refilling is a problem.

You can buy or rent extension poles for higher paint work. These poles sometimes enable you to do the painting from the ground or from a low scaffold, eliminating the need for high ladders and several tiers of scaffolding.

You can buy throwaway brushes and pads for very little money. The idea is that you can use the brush or pad for a day or so and then throw it into the garbage rather than clean it up.

Before you begin painting, have the surface as clean and dry as possible. Trapped moisture can cause blistering or bubbling later and you might have to repeat the job. Paint with the grain whenever possible. Siding made of vinyl or aluminum will not have a grain, but you should paint along the long surface. For vertical siding, paint up and down. For siding installed horizontally, paint from left and right. Wood grains are different. Paint shingles or shakes vertically and board siding in the direction of the grain, especially if you are using a brush. If you use a roller, you can paint cross-grain better but you still get smoother and better surface covering if you follow the grain. Whether you are painting or rolling, always lap the last strokes or passes by an inch or two. This eliminates the lap marks that are so noticeable in many paint jobs.

If the surface is very porous, as with blocks, you will need to apply a sealer before you apply paint. Whether you are using a roller, brush, or pad, when painting porous materials load the brush or roller to the drip point and apply firm pressure to force the paint into all pores and tiny holes and crevices. You need to be as concerned about sealing as you are about looks. If there are pinholes where paint does not cover, insects and moisture can penetrate and cause damage later.

When you select stains, remember that you will not conceal the natural grains of the surface; you will only change the hues or tints. Inform your dealer of the type of wood you plan to stain and ask his advice about which stains will produce the best waterproofing and sealant actions and which will look better when the job is done. Many dealers have several samples of various woods that have been painted or stained. If you have oak shingles, do not be content with looking at the samples of pine stained with the stain you plan to buy. Ask to see how the stain looks on oak or whatever wood you intend to cover.

Glossary

aggregate Gravel, sand, or similar material used in cement or mortar. Course, or common-weight, aggregates, such as stone or gravel, are the heaviest materials. Fine, or lightweight, aggregates are masonry sand or river sand.

ashler stone See stone.

baluster The square or turned stair component that supports the stair rail.

barnboard Term given to rough-sawn or rough-hewn siding with one irregular edge.

baseline The point where the wall unit meets the foundation wall.

batten Strip of wood placed across a surface to cover joints.

bed joint See joint.

block, cap Solid concrete block that is laid flat on a concrete block wall or similar surface.

bond Adhesion or tying together various components of a masonry unit with mortar or reinforcement devices.

bond, common Method of bricklaying where bricks are laid end to end lengthwise along a course and include a row of headers.

bond, English Method of bricklaying with alternating courses of stretchers and headers.

bond, Flemish Method of bricklaying in which courses of stretchers and headers are laid one beside the other.

bond, running Method of bricklaying with bricks laid end to end lengthwise along a course.

bond, stack Method of bricklaying in which courses consist of either all stretchers or headers and with all vertical joints aligned.

bracing, let-in Wood braces of 2-×-4 lengths that are angle cut and run from the sole plate to the top plate of wall framing.

buttering Placing mortar on a masonary unit with a trowel in order to form a joint.

cap block   See block.

channel, F   One of two anchor points for siding panels.

channel, J   Metal structure designed to receive ends of siding panels at corner posts.

chinking, vinyl   Plastic material used between components of log structures.

common bond   See bond.

concrete, fiber   See fiber.

connector, slip-joint   Metal slot allowing one length of guttering to fit into another.

course aggregate   See aggregate.

cube   A unit of 90 concrete blocks.

double-coursing   Method of nailing up two layers of material, usually refers to shingles.

English bond   See bond.

fascia   Wooden piece used for the outside face of a box cornice located at the ends of rafters and lookouts.

F-channel   See channel.

ferrule   Metal piece that slips over the spikes inside guttering troughs.

fiber concrete   Non-asbestos concrete sections or boards used as siding.

fine aggregate   See aggregate.

flashing   Any of various metals used in the bed joint of a chimney-roof juncture that prevents moisture from entering under roofing materials. *Head flashing* refers to material used to prevent moisture from entering between joint units.

Flemish bond   See bond.

footing   The base, or bottom, of a structure, usually concrete.

foundation wall   The supporting structure below the first-floor level of construction.

framing square   Construction tool used for marking square cuts and for squaring corners.

froe   Cutting tool with a long, thick blade that is sharp on the bottom and flat on the top.

furring strip   Narrow strip of wood used to form a nailing base for another surface.

header   In masonry, a unit laid over two walls to tie them together.

head flashing   See flashing.

insulation   Any of various materials used to slow the passage of air.

J-channel   See channel.

jointing   Finishing method of pressing mortar or concrete into the joints of masonry units.

joint, bed   Masonry joint where blocks join end to end with one block laid on top of another.

joist   One of several beams used to support floor or ceiling loads which, in turn, is supported by a larger timber.

lath strip   Any of various materials attached to a building frame to serve as a plaster base.

lattice   Crisscross strips, usually wood or vinyl, installed in sections.

let-in bracing   See bracing.

line level   Small level that can be attached to a chalk line to ensure levelness when making construction markings.

lintel   Length of metal that is laid into a mortar bed and crosses windows and doors to support overhead loads.

mortar bed   Continuous band of mortar placed on footings or on the tops of brick rows as a basis for a new course of bricks.

nail hole punch   See punch.

oriented strand board (OSB)   Pressed wood type of sheathing.

pargeting   Masonry process consisting of spreading a layer of thin mortar over the entire surface of a wall or other masonry structure.

particleboard   A bonded panel of particles, usually wood shavings, and a resin or some other type of binder.

partition stud   Wooden or metal member of a wall.

perch (of stone)   Measure of about 25 cubic feet of stone.

plate, sole   Timber that forms the bottom of the wall frame.

plate, top   Timber that covers the tops of the studs of a wall frame.

plywood   Sheathing composed of thin layers of wood glued and pressed in alternate, crossing layers.

punch, nail hole   Tool used to create elongated holes in the cut edge of a vinyl panel.

punch, snap lock   Tool used to punch tabs in trimmed vinyl panels.

quoin   Solid exterior angle in masonry construction.

R-rating   Number specifying the efficiency of insulation.

rubble stone   See stone.

running bond   See bond.

shakes, hand-split and resawn   Shakes with hand-split faces or with hand-split look and backs that are resawn.

shakes, straight-split   Shakes made by a craftsman and split straight rather than tapered.

shakes, taper-split   Shakes made by a craftsman using a froe at an angle resulting in a tapered shape.

sheathing   Any of several available materials used to face the outside of a wood-studded wall.

shim   Small strip of wood used to level wood members.

shingles, surface   Shingles that will show when work is done, also called top shingles.

slip-joint connectors   See connectors.

snap lock punch   See punch.

soffit   Underside of an overhang or similar structure of a building.

sole plate   See plate.

spike   A long, nail-shaped metal piece used to support guttering troughs.

spline   Narrow strip, usually wood but sometimes metal, that fits into a groove or slot of components to form a joint.

stack bond   See bond.

starter strip Wooden length of 2×4 that runs along a wall line where framing meets the foundation wall and provides a watershed structure.

stone, ashlar Stone that is squared and cut to resemble uniform blocks of essentially the same shape and size.

stone, rubble Stone left in its natural shape.

story pole Device used by carpenters and masons to ensure proper alignment of wall courses.

stretchers Bricks laid end to end lengthwise in a course.

strip, furring See furring.

strip, watershed See watershed.

stucco Decorating finish in masonry construction where a plasticlike cement mixture is applied to walls.

stud An upright in a wall frame of a building to which insulating or finishing panels are nailed.

stud, common See common.

stud, partition See partition.

top plate See plate.

vapor barrier Any of various watertight materials used to prevent moisture from entering a structure.

vertical sheathing See sheathing.

waferboard Layered wood type of sheathing, in same family as OSB.

wall tie Metal strip used to bind masonry units to wood-framed walls.

watershed strip Narrow strip, usually wooden, installed at the bottom of a wall line to produce a watershed effect for siding.

wrapping Plastic material used on the sides of a structure to keep air from infiltrating and causing heating or cooling loss.

Index